# Russia

Vincenzo Berghella

Copyright Page

Copyright year: 2013

ISBN No:

**From the same author:** (see also )

- **Obstetric Evidence Based Guidelines.** Informa Healthcare, London, UK, and New York, USA (2007) [English]

- **Maternal Fetal Evidence Based Guidelines.** Informa Healthcare, London, UK, and New York, USA (2007 )[English]

- **Laughter, the best medicine. Jokes for everyone.** (2007) [English]

- **Ridere, la migliore medicina. Barzellette per bambini.** (2007) [Italiano]

- **My favorite quotes.** (2009) [English]

- **In medio stat virtus – Citazioni d'autore.** (2009) [Italiano]

- **Quello che di voi vive in me.** (2009) [Italiano]

- **Dall'altra parte dell'oceano.** (2010) [Italiano] [Translated in: **On the other side of the ocean** (2013) [English]

- **Preterm Birth: Prevention and Management.** Wiley-Blackwell. Oxford, United Kingdom. (2010) [English]

- **From father to son.** (2010) [English]

- **Sollazzi.** (2010) [Italiano]

- **The land of religions.** (2011) [English] [Translated in: **La terra dell'amore** (2013) [Italiano]

- **Giramondo.** (2011) [Italiano]

- **Obstetric Evidence Based Guidelines.** Informa Healthcare, London, UK, and New York, USA (2012; Second Edition)[English]

- **Maternal Fetal Evidence Based Guidelines.** Informa Healthcare, London, UK, and New York, USA (2012; Second Edition)[English]

- **Trip to London.** (2012) [English]

- **Il primo amore non si scorda mai.** (2012) [Italiano]

- **Maldives.** (2013) [English]

# Travel brings peace

(Heard from a Turkish guy on a flight from Istanbul to London)

# Preparations

It's a wonderful period of my life. Undeservingly, I get invited several times a year to attend some of the best medical scientific world conferences in my academic field of interest, maternal-fetal medicine. The invitation to Russia came in August, 2011. I received an email from Prof. Zulfiya Khodzhaeva saying, "On behalf of the Russian Society of Obstetricians and Gynecologists we would like to invite you as a guest speaker to the Russian Congress "Mother and Child" that will take place in Moscow on September 28-30th." Unfortunately I could not attend that conference, due to prior engagements. When she re-invited me for May 2013, eight months in advance, this revealed itself as a period I could travel, given both my partners in Philadelphia would be at work.

In fact, I also received an invitation to go to Moscow for another international conference in June, 2013, which I declined. The reasons were several: the May period was better for my schedule; the organization of the May congress seemed to be impeccable; these were both a completely different organization and people I had not interacted with before and was interested in knowing; and the Russian professor stated she had heard me speak at the FIGO (International Federation of Obstetricians and Gynecologists) conference in Rome, Italy, in October 2012, and so I was sure this was a true invitation, by colleagues who held me in high esteem.

The Russian organizers are in fact extremely kind, helpful, understanding. I ask for a visit to Saint Petersburg, as I had always heard a visit to Russia has to include at least both Moscow, the current capital, and the city founded by Peter the Great, the old tsar capital. I ask for guided tours in both cities. I even ask for help booking further stops in Rome, Italy, and Istanbul, Turkey, where I have another two talks. The Russian organizers not only book all the six flights for my entire trip, but even pay for the whole thing, despite my volunteering to foot the bill for the extras. Most of the flying is in business class, and all with great airlines. My hotels in Russia are all 5-star hotels.

So, Elena Chukhnova, who I thought worked for a travel agency, but in fact later in Russia I learned worked for a pharmaceutical company called Besins Healthcare, was always punctual to answer all my emails, requests, and suggestions. Preparations for the trips started to unfold. Unfortunately, given the end of school time of year, my wife and my two sons Andrea and Pietro could not come with me. I even tried with my parents and siblings in Italy, but they also could not accompany me.

There was a major glitch in the preparations for the trip. About a month before the scheduled departure for Moscow, I received from Elena email attachments regarding my hotels and official invitation documents, mostly in Cyrillic. The email asked me to get a visa, using the materials I had just received. A visa? This was the first time I realize I need a visa. I have visited dozens of countries in many continents, and very rarely needed a visa.

So I started right away obtaining information from the web, from Elena, and from calling directly the Russian Embassy in Washington. The summary of hours of data gathering was that it was easiest to request a visa as an American citizen, for as an Italian I would have also needed medical clearance. The Russian Embassy worried me quite a bit: in May there were several Russian national holidays, and offices therefore would be closed. I was quickly running out of time. Usually it took 3-4 weeks to get a visa.

Panicked, when I asked for advice, the Russian Embassy suggested I use a paid service. There were many I could choose from, one of them, they said, was INVISA. I went online, found INVISA, and quickly called their Washington headquarters. Another kind lady, with a similar Russian accent as the one of the nice lady of the Russian Embassy, answered. She confirmed the information I already had, added some more, but then, when I asked for direct help, she floored me. With a departure date within a month, they could not help me, they were too busy. May be I could try another company, or the Russian Embassy, or one of the Consulates.

I began to call and email frantically other companies, with no success. In the meanwhile, I had the documentation ready. I also tried the Russian Consulate in New York, the closest to Philadelphia. They never answered the phone, and their hours were horrific, plus I did not want to lose time at work.

Finally, I got a small breakthrough: the INVISA office in Boston answered. Again, a friendly Russian lady. She told me that for sure I was still in time, to send everything to the New York INVISA office which was the one that served Philadelphian, and relax. Relax? I must have called the INVISA office in New York over ten times, at all times of day, without ever an answer. Three emails had also gone without a single reply. The Boston agent reassured that there were just busy, not to worry.

At this point I had only two options: drive to New York and chance the Russian Consulate, or send a package, including my beloved USA passport, to INVISA. The thought of going to New York and wait forever, with the chance to have missing documents, or to be told I'm too late, or to be treated rudely as I've often been treated in Consulates around the world, including American Consulates when I was not a citizen, was not appealing.

Thankfully, the New York INVISA office, at 4pm one afternoon, in the last desperate call, answered. "Sure, we are open, send all materials, we'll get you a visa." An hour later, my huge package, in English and Cyrillic, with over 30 pages of documents, and official Russian Embassy on-line application, as well as my USA passport, left my office FedEx for INVISA, in New York.

Then, silence again. My wonderful, irreplaceable assistant Lynn checked online and reported 'they' had received the package. But I had no idea if it was complete, if they still thought I had a good chance at getting a visa, if and/or when I would get it. The Russian Congress organizers had spent surely close to five figures for my trip. Would it all go to waste?

I also could not get much in the mood for the trip, with the continuous uncertainty. No visa, no trip. I usually read in detail the history of the new country I'm about to visit. I buy and read a book, and at least one guide. I delayed doing this, a bit superstitiously.

Moreover, this ordeal made me feel like the cold war was still going on. I'm a bit afraid, thinking about traveling by myself in what I grew up hearing as the evil empire, the adversary. For the first time in my life, after visiting over thirty foreign countries in five continents, I was having trouble obtaining the right to travel.

Eventually, after several tries, I got the Russian lady at INVISA New York back on the phone. Yes, they had received my package. Yes, everything was complete. Yes, she had submitted it to the Russian Consulate in New York, and they had told her to expect my passport back with the visa on it on or before May 16. This was five days before my scheduled flight to Russia, but the agent reassured me, 'not to worry.'

About ten days before the scheduled departure, I eventually gave in, and bought and started reading, trying not to get too excited, the FODOR's guide to Moscow and Saint Petersburg, and 'A history of Russia,' by Nicholas Riasanovsky and Mark Steinberg, a textbook with the best reputation as the ultimate resource on the subject.

I also study one of the Berghella's favorite books, 'The 1,000 places to visit before you die.' In Moscow, they recommend three places: Red Square and Kremlin; the Bolshoi theatre (near Red Square); and the Tretyakov Gallery (full of Kandinskys and Chagalls), with the Moscow Metro. In Saint Petersburg, the five recommendations are for the White Night festival (which is in June, so I'll miss it); the Winter Palace; the Hermitage; and, just outside the city, Catherine Palace and Pavlovsk Palace; as well as the Peterhof, another famous tsar palace. I know I may miss the gallery in Moscow, and the palaces outside of Saint Petersburg given the short trips full of lectures, but I plan to focus on the rest, which is plenty.

May 15 came and went. May 16 came, and, when I failed to receive any package, I called INVISA. I eventually got a live voce, the familiar lady with an unpronounceable name. She checked. Nothing had arrived. She would call the Russian Consulate, inquire, and call me back in 5-10 minutes. Of course, I did not receive any more calls from her that day.

The next day, I got through, and was told my visa was getting done, and would arrive at INVISA in a day, to then be sent to me the same day by UPS. I told the whole office at work, to be alert. And then I followed online every stop and progress of the desired package.

The package, with my passport and a three-by-four-inch Russian visa on one of its pages, arrived in my office in Philadelphia at about 4pm on May 20, 2013, about 26 hours before my flight for London and then Moscow, scheduled to leave on May 21, 2013, at 6pm. What an ordeal. It was Winston Churchill who said, in1939, that Russia is "a riddle, wrapped in a mystery, inside an enigma." I was afraid this may be still true. I remained hopeful my Russian hosts would make my stay in Russia easier than getting the visa.

# The flight over

The flight over, unlike the visa, could not be more pleasant. Life is good. I'm flying business class on British Airways first from Philadelphia to London, and then London to Moscow. I brought only a red carry-on, and a backpack. Enough clothes to last me 5-6 days, before then getting them cleaned in Pescara, Italy, at home with my mother and her Pilipino help, the wonderful Karen, after this Russian trip.

I've already checked in online, so in Philadelphia I go directly to the gate, skipping all lines given the business class status. At the gate, the extremely nice woman urges me to go to the VIP Lounge. The lounge of course is nice, comfortable, and has good Wi-Fi. I eat some fruit, store a couple of more apples in my backpack, and check emails. A soft speaker announces at 5:30pm that preferred seating is ready to board.

I board the flight, and we leave on time, at 18:10 on May 21$^{st}$.
After a sumptuous three-course meal, I manage to sleep about 2 to 3 of the less than 6 hours of flying, completely reclined like in a bed. In London, the only trouble is that my deodorant, almost empty but in a 112mL bottle, does not pass the London Airport Security – the limit indeed is 100mL - and gets confiscated. In my long experience, this is maybe only the second time ever this kind of bottle does not pass security. In fact, nobody said anything when I left Philadelphia. But I do not argue at all.

In the same terminal 5 where I arrived in Heathrow, after spending some time again in the VIP lounge, I board the business class trip to Moscow, which leaves on time at 08:50am, on May 22$^{nd}$.

Unlike other trips, so far this one has not familiarized me yet with the Russian culture or people. There are only about eight passengers in business class from Heathrow to Domodedovo, one of the Moscow's airports, and one of the largest in the world. I hear no Russian being spoken. The British Airways pilots and staff are all British. They are so ever nice. My friend Paolo is right to rave about British Airways, the staff is superb, friendly, and they make you feel like a king. They read your mind, and anticipate every wish, making it soon come true with a smile.

This flight, I do not wait for the meal, but soon after takeoff I level my seat to make it a flat bed, and get another 2 to 3 hours of deep sleep, warm under two thick comforters.

Fittingly, there are thick clouds over Moscow, and while at 39,000 feet there is the sun, the captain on the flight announces heavy rain down on the ground in Moscow.

## May 22, in Moscow

We land in Moscow on time, at 15.30. I get through customs without any problems, using my USA passport with the special, and bravely-obtained, Russian visa, which the officer quickly glances at. I have no luggage to pick up, as I just traveled with a carry-on, and a back-pack which I borrowed from one of my sons.

My instructions, four single-line pages of details mostly from Elena but also from my own notes, said that 'a driver will meet you with the nameplate «Berghella» and transfer you to the hotel «Golden Ring».' I do not see the driver initially, and worry for about 10 seconds. But then, after I'm through most of the crowd, we do find each other. He speaks English pretty well, is courteous but a bit rough. As most Russians, he has what Americans would say are dressy formal pants and shirt, and leather belt and shoes.

As we step out of the airport building towards the parking lot and his car, he says with an heavy accent that 'where we are walking now there was a river just a few minutes ago,' referring to the heavy rain that just ended. We need no umbrella – I do have brought one small foldable one with me. He announces that the traffic is terrible in Moscow, and it will take more than one hour to get to the hotel. I'm in no rush, and there is no need to complain.

The car trip is overall pleasant. I'm sufficiently awake to enjoy the sight of a place I've never visited before. Under the clouds, we do see lots of green vegetation and trees. Overall though, grey is the dominant color and feeling through my visit in Moscow. My chauffer is a slow driver, and is listening to 89.1FM, a smooth jazz radio channel, with American music. On the road, I do notice some, but only very few - less than 5% - old-looking, Soviet-era cars, similar to FIAT 128's from 40 years ago. Later I'll realize these are Ladas, Russian-made cars based on the FIAT 1966 sedan model124. Over 20 million units have been sold, making it the highest-selling automobile to be produced without major design change. In general, though, Muscovites are driving modern cars, mostly Japanese as well as plenty of BMW and Mercedes.

As we get closer to town, a Soviet-style tram, all metallic, electric, goes by, but for the rest, the country appears pretty modern. I do notice some Mussolini-type buildings, but many appear to be similar to public housing common in the 60's and 70's in most European capitals. The roads we travel on are wide. In fact, approaching downtown Moscow, at one point I notice 10 lanes each way, a wider road than in California!

I do see on the way a building with the sickle and hammer old communist sign, so feared by us in the West during the cold war era. The two tools are symbols of the industrial proletariat and the peasantry; placing them together symbolizes the unity between industrial and agricultural workers. This emblem was conceived during the 1917 Russian Revolution. It was part of the red flag of the Soviet Union, and is still part of the red flag of the Chinese Communist Party.

The travel guidebook had suggested learning the characters of the Russian alphabet, to be able to decipher signs. Given the fact I studied ancient Greek for five years, and am fluent in both Latin-derived and Anglo-Saxon-derived languages, I try to decode what I see from the car window. The first one is АУШАН, which I can translate to Auchan, the European megastore chain. The second is Heinz КЕТЧУП, or ketchup. Guessing at what's written in Cyrillic is quite a fun game. After seeing it many times, I finally decipher the rebus of the СТОП sign I see under every light at intersections: it means 'Stop.'

I get to hotel not before about 6pm. It's the Golden Ring Hotel, a 5-start hotel on 5 Smolenskaya Street. As I check in, the front desk keeps my passport to verify it. I hope they do not misplace it, and do not lose a pass, consisting of a small flimsy piece of paper mostly in Cyrillic, which they gave me at passport control at the airport.

But my main issue is that my iPhone does not work. I seem not to be able to get any reception. After such a long trip, I know my wife in Philadelphia, and my mother and father in Pescara, are eager to hear from me. I struggle for quite a while, emailing my assistant Lynn at Thomas Jefferson University in Philadelphia, where I work, for help.

After about four emails, and countless 'power off; power on,' as well as 'telephone card out; telephone card in' tries, at least the cellular phone connection finds by roaming a Russian line for me to reassure family, and me, as I finally feel I'm not disconnected from them.

In between cell phone checks, over half an hour after my arrival, I return to the entrance of the hotel and get back my passport from concierge. I also get about 5,000 rubles – 30 rubles are about a dollar - from the money machine with my PNC Bank card. Very easy. Cell phone working, rubles in pocket, and luggage contents organized in the hotel room, I'm ready now to go out and walk around. My plan from the organizers for this evening is 'free time.'

I know the hotel is not far from center, I'm told about a 30-minute walk by the huge guard in front of the entrance. He points me to the right of the hotel, and then to the left, and then again the right, straight. All by sign signals, as his English stops at 'hello.' My Wi-Fi connection on the cell phone does not work, so I cannot use Google Maps to figure out my route. I'm forced to memorize the route I'm taking, often looking behind myself to be able to recognize the streets on my way back.

From the paper map of Moscow, and later from the explanations of my guides, Moscow seems to be organized around a center, which is the Kremlin. At least three different sets of protective walls were built, at different times, around it. One, which is still intact, is immediately around it. Another one is about a kilometer around it. And then another more peripheral one is about two kilometers around it, forming an almost perfect circle.

Both of these two sets of outer walls have, through the centuries, pretty much disappeared, substituted by large boulevards. The inner one is called the Boulevard Ring, and is not a complete circle, because its base is the Moscow River, on the bank of which the Kremlin was built. The other circle is now the Garden Ring, the complete bigger circle. It's called Garden because originally it was lined by many trees, which are now gone. My hotel is on the west side, right on the Garden Ring.

A lot of the above geographical information is still unknown to me as I venture out for the first time. One of the buildings I notice immediately, only about 30 yards from the hotel, is a huge Soviet-era skyscraper, probably about 30 stories high, with plenty of sickle and hammer signs still on it. Only now, studying more details to write this book, I realize is the Russian Foreign Ministry building.

Now on the Garden Ring, called here Novinsky Boulevard, I continue straight, as indicated to me by the hotel guard. Street signs are very few and far between, and in Cyrillic only. So I keep on asking other pedestrians for directions, with a friendly 'Kremlin?' To my amazement, most persons I ask stare at me like I'm speaking a language from the moon. How can it be that both young and old Muscovites do not know where the Kremlin is? Especially since I must be at only less than a mile from it?

Later on I'm told Kremlin is pronounced differently in Russian, so that goes the mystery. Nonetheless, some do understand it, and point me in the right direction, which mostly involves turning right at the next huge boulevard, called Novy Arbat (or New Arbat in English), which by my map seems to show going straight towards the center of town and my goal.

In the meanwhile, I pass modern shops, tall new buildings, even a Penthouse Club and а Макдоналдс (MacDonald's). On the street, there are many beautiful tall girls, slim, with light eyes, often shaped like almonds and pointing up on the outside. Most women wear nice, fancy shoes, with high heels, and walk straight up like princesses.

I go through a couple of underpasses, then on the left a typical Russian Christian Orthodox church and a very large supermarket, and then on the right what I later realize is the oldest Moscow movie theatre. I end up in a square where there is a large Greek-temple like building, with a large, about 12-foot tall, statue.

On the top of the classical building, one can see, after 'decoding' from the bold Cyrillic letters, the inscription ΛЕННHA (Lenina). So I assume the large statue is of Lenin, as it is one of a bold man, in a pose somewhat similar to Rodin's 'the thinker,' similar to other Lenin's statues that I've seen in books. A pigeon is happily standing on top of the bold head. Only later I'll realize the building is the Russian State Library, once called Biblioteca Imemi Lenina (in honor of Lenin), and the statue is of Dostoyevsky. Many other famous novelists, such as Tolstoy, have busts on the façade and side of the building, which houses Russia's biggest library.

Fedor Dostoyevsky lived from 1821 to 1881, and was even imprisoned in Siberia for his writings. He represented the most Russian of writers, even if he was international and human as a master in deep psychology. His late novels Crime and Punishment, The Idiot, The Possessed, and Brother Karamazov are some of the best ever written. Count Lev Tolstoy was born to a noble family in 1828. His best known works are War and Peace of 1869, and Anna Karenina of 1876. Search of true love in a corrupt and violent society were often his themes, stressing the everyday practice of moral good.

Another underpass to go below another main road, and I'm in front of large walls. Inside it, I realize, it's the Kremlin. I ask around, and get to the ticket office, which has by now closed for the day: I won't be able to get in tonight. But an helpful Muscovite tells me, when asked, that I can definitively get to the Red Square, just about a hundred yard in front of me, following the walls, along the nice park, and then right up a small incline.

I begin to realize the Kremlin is not what I thought it was. I always envisioned it as one scary-looking building where mean men plotted evil schemes. Or such Italian and US TV would make you believe, especially in the 70's when I was growing up. Instead, the Kremlin is a fortress, inside which there are many different buildings. *Kreml* means 'citadel' or 'fortress.' The first myths begin to unravel.

I have not eaten yet, and, while on my right I continue to have the Kremlin's walls, on the left, past a large fountain, I spot a few food stores. The most prominent are a MacDonald's, and a Sbarro's Pizza. I get two slices of pizza, and a bottle of water. The Russian checkout girl asks me several times for change other than a 500-rubles bill, but that's all I have. Behind her, a sign advertises a concert by the Pooh, an Italian pop music band that was most popular back home in the 70's. Apparently, Russians still love Italian music from that period.

With the bag with food and water in hand, I head up towards what I'm told is the Red Square. I sit down on a ledge, and devour the two large slices, while sipping some water. In the meanwhile, I explore the large plaza, where so much history has happened.

On my left, there is a huge Renaissance building, quite classical in its look, not too dissimilar from the Louvre's architecture. This is the GUM, pronounced 'goom', whose initials stand for Glavnyi Universalny Magazin, or 'Main Universal Store,' literally, a huge emporium built in 1889-93 and now house to magnificent modern stores; it's a mall! It was Catherine II of Russia who originally commissioned Giacomo Quarenghi, a Neoclassical architect from Italy, to design a huge trade center along the east side of Red Square, which was later rebuilt after a fire.

As any main square in any major (or even minor) city, Red Square was originally a market (in fact its originally name was Torg, which means marketplace in Slavonic). In front, quite far, there is a large stage begin set up, or dismantled, I can't tell. On my right, the walls of the Kremlin, with a low reddish building in front.

The name Red Square comes neither from the color of the bricks around it nor from the link between the color red and communism. Rather, the name came about because the Russian word красная (krasnaya) can mean either 'red' or 'beautiful.' This word, with the meaning 'beautiful,' was originally applied to Saint Basil's Cathedral and was subsequently transferred to the nearby square. The bright red stars on top of the Kremlin building are impressive, and still very much Soviet-style.

Moscow was founded here around the 12th century. To summarize the history of Russia before Moscow's founding, Russia's more recent history can start when the ruler Oleg occupied Kiev on the Dnieper in 882 and founded the first state, the Kievan Rus. So, in a sense, Russia started as Ukraine, and Ukraine is more ancient a state than Russia, as well as a ruler over early Russia.

Tables 1 and 2 on pages 78-79, at the end of the book, from the eight edition of the History of Russia by Nicholas V. Riasanovsky and Mark D. Steinberg, Oxford University Press 2011, covers the story of Russia's rulers from Oleg, to the death of Ivan the Terrible in 1584.

Oleg's grandson, Vladimir, adopted Christianity from Constantinople around 988. So Christianity came to Russia from Byzantium, not from Rome. When the break between the Eastern and

Western Churches occurred in 1054, Russia continued to be a follower of the Eastern traditions, which in fact it sustained even more than Constantinople, which was converted to Islam after being taken over by the Ottomans in 1453.

In the 15th century, Moscow emerged as the heart of the newly unified Russia. By the 16th century, it was the capital of the huge new empire of Russia. Peter the Great, in 1703, decided to move the capital to a new city, founded by him to be closer to Europe and therefore follow more closely its influence: St Petersburg. Tsars started living in St Petersburg, but continued to get crowned and buried here. Moscow regained its role of capital of Russia in 1917, when the Bolshevik revolution brought out of the city of the tsars, St Petersburg, and back to Moscow, the more proletarian town, the power of government.

The weather is cloudy, and it's beginning to get a bit chilly, so I put on a sweater over my shirt and, after about twenty-five minutes of pure enjoyment and meditation alone with my thoughts in Red Square, I head back down, with the plan to return to the hotel, if I can figure out the route.

But as I enter the park near the walls, the first drops of rain, and soon a fierce thunderstorm break out. I run for cover, which I find under an awning in a nearby square. There are about ten other people with me; two, a young boy and a girl, kiss continuously, which is a common site in Moscow. I love it. Other locals instead are seen running quickly towards their destination. Some, young and unfazed by the rain, just walk under it.

I figure this thunderstorm will pass soon. But it does not. I do not have the umbrella with me. I move from awning to awning trying to figure out when the rain will stop. My cell is not working; I have no reception, so I'm completely isolated. A huge rainbow appears over the Kremlin, soon to double itself, which I take, in many different ways, as a good omen. Nonetheless, the heavy rain, even with the rainbows, lasts for about an interminable hour. I get soaking wet.

Eventually the rain subsides, and soon stops. I take off the wet sweater, and walk my way back with just my shirt. But it is not too cold, and, despite being past 9pm, it is still light out.

I get back to the hotel around 10pm, delayed a lot on my plans for an early night. I first have to warm up. Once I take my soaked socks off, I notice both my feet are black from my shoes, a pair of old dark blue Clarks, which have stained when all wet. I plug in my iPhone and MacBook Air, with European adapters I had brought with me. Past 11pm, I'm in bed, comfortable.

I do wake up at 4:40am Moscow's time, because of the jet lag, an 8-hour difference (in Philadelphia it would be 8:40pm of the day before). I toss and turn for over an hour. Then the alarm goes off at 8:30am when I'm in deep sleep. I wonder why did I set it up for 8:30am? Not enough time to sleep my 8 hours, given that I did not sleep the mid part of the night. And not enough time to really take a stroll outside, as I needed to get picked up by 10:45am.

## May 23, Thursday

All these 5-star hotels have comfortable beds, fancy smooth linens, huge bathrooms, bright white bathrobes, slippers, shoe cleaners, free bottled waters, and any other amenities you can think of. The morning is a pleasure. Breakfast is on the second floor, in a wide room with more food than anyone can imagine. A fancily dressed blond woman is playing a harp, and the gentle sound sooths the atmosphere.

I end up staying in hotel room until 10:45 am, the time that I am supposed to get picked up. I do not have enough time to walk around, as originally planned, and it was also raining a bit. After breakfast, I check emails, but spend most time practicing the lecture I am supposed to give at the Russian Congress in a few hours. Thankfully I do not change my plan, and keep it to about 60 slides.

As per plan, at 10:45am a driver meets me, again with the now familiar but always a bit different nameplate «Berghella», on the reception of the hotel for transfer to the congress venue: the Kulakov Scientific Center of Obstetrics, Gynecology and Perinatology, on Oparina Street. The driver is a fat man who speaks no English, but he is courteous. As we step out of the hotel, three red military guards cross in front of me, like in a parade on Red Square.

On the way, towards the less central quartiers of this city of twenty million, the driver is also listening to smooth jazz 89.1. I realize it must be the company's orders, impossible that all Russian chauffeurs like the same music. Some areas we go through look grey like East Berlin. There is lots of traffic again, and I again try to kill time by trying to decider signs. Even СТАРБАКС КОФЕ, or Starbucks Coffee, is in Cyrillic.

I know figure out that the few old looking cars are called Lada, mostly '2015' (the type) sedans, while some are '2014,' while the station wagons are '2104.' I feel a bit like a fancy packaged gift being delivered, with my red tie around my neck like a red ribbon. Around me, the surroundings seem not dissimilar from the EXPO area in Rome called EUR. The car I'm on is very nice again, yesterday a Volvo, today a BMW, with GPS, a rear view camera, and all the perks. I feel again over-spoiled, unmeritoriously so.

I'm let off by the driver right in front of the main entrance of the place where I'll give the talk. Waiting for me, on the sidewalk, is finally at least somebody I've previously corresponded with. Elena Chukhnova is probably at least 5'10", taller with the high heels and fancy shoes, and is wearing a tight bright pinkish dress that raps her generous curves tight. She has a decorative tiny white jacket on top, clearly for fashion and not for warmth.

As we walk into the conference center of the health facility, Elena explains to me that there are three lecture halls. I will lecture in the biggest one. I tell her I would like to put my slides in their computer, and make sure everything works. As I wait for her to find out how the program is going and if I'll be lecturing as scheduled around 12:15pm, I roam around. There are a few medical bookstands, and to my absolute amazement, one is selling my own medical textbooks, Obstetric Evidence Based Guidelines, and Maternal Fetal Evidence Based Guidelines. In fact, she has both the first, much discounted, and the second editions!

In a VIP room where I get served tea, and offered all kinds of sweets, the translator asks me a bit about the contents of my lecture, on 'Prevention of Preterm Birth using Cervical Length Screening and different progestagens,' the topic I'm most famous for. She actually wants to understand the subject well, so to be able to translate it appropriately. Elena tells me the interpreter is indeed a pediatrician by training.

During my hour-long talk, the interpreter is standing right next to me, and translates every sentence. I even say at some point I'm honored that the translator is a pediatrician. She hesitates after I pause so she can translate this. When I hear the second of silence and hesitation, I turn around to her, who is just a step behind me with a standing pole and microphone, and mimic to her with my right hand to translate that, too. She does, a bit embarrassed.

She will tell me later that "You are the best speaker I ever had to translate for." All I did is follow her instructions, and point to her where I was on the slides while I talked. After the applause, I get asked about ten questions, from both the audience in general, and the moderator, Professor Zulfiya Khodzhaeva.

I'm then taken around the hospital by some of the physicians, all in their thirties or younger. Some parts, especially the outpatient clinics, are quite modern. There are patients everywhere. The labor and delivery ward, while less recently built, seems adequate, but there are few private rooms, at least to my assessment. The anesthesia machines in the cesarean delivery room also seem a bit, but not much, out of date compared to the US. Overall, I see it as a very safe place to have a baby.

Interestingly, to get through the three floors where ob-gyn is mainly housed, we have to go through stairs, as there is no public elevator. So even pregnant patients need to climb stairs to get to Labor & Delivery. My guides say this is how it was everywhere in the Soviet era.

Interestingly enough, I'm told >90% of physicians in Russia are women, 'it's a woman's profession.' At the end of the hospital and clinics tour, I'm taken to the huge, modern office of the University boss, a bold robust man in his late 50's or early 60's. He lets me sit in a chair near him, but at least six inches at a lower level than his own chair.

He lavishly compliments me in front of a small crowd. He also makes sure he mentions he was last week with the Russian Health Secretary and the US counterpart, apparently a good friend of Hillary Clinton. A bit of name dropping. In the library behind him I do notice the 2nd editions of my two evidence-based books. He gives me a Russian present for memento, and we take ceremonial pictures.

It's now past 2pm. With Elena Chukhnova, and the translator, we go finally for lunch, not far from the congress venue, with traditional Caucasian cuisine. Elena takes off her heels to drive to the restaurant, as she has flat shoes in the car just for driving. The traffic is again intense, so it takes us about 20 minutes for about 5 miles.

The restaurant has wooden tables and chairs outside, and, since it's not raining and it must be in the upper 60's, I say, when asked, that I'd prefer to seat outside. The kind waiter brings each of us three a wool cover, to put over our shoulders. But after five minutes I take it off, as it's not that cold, and I'm quite comfortable with just my shirt.

I get to know my two partners for lunch a bit better. The translator, the pediatrician, Elena Shubina, is from Vladivostok, so we talk about the Far East and Siberia for a while. Elena is from Moscow, with her father originally from Central Asia, which in Russia means east of Moscow but west of the Urals. We talk about how big Russia is, still one seventh of all Earth. They are very happy that I'm going to St Petersburg.

When asked for preferences, I tell them they could order whatever they want, the most special Caucasian foods. Elena is quite happy to order what seemed to me to be many different dishes. To drink, I have what Elena ordered in a carafe, which is a berry drink, similar to cranberries. We start with a large slice of eggplant, completely covered by a thick creamy sauce, which looks like a pure' of tuna, but tasted even better. The two Elenas explained to me that it was made of grated nuts.

Then we continue with a white pizza, with cheese on top and inside. Then we have an oval pie, certainly baked in a wood oven, with in the middle a small egg, oil, and a tiny piece of butter still intact, as is the red eye – the yolk - of the egg. The waiter mixes this pool of ingredients inside the valley made in the flour focaccia, and tells us all to share it, by carving out with our hands pieces of it from the crusty perimeter. It is delicious, even if a simple treat.

Then we are served what I guess is the main course, which consists of three different kinds of meat. We have three meatballs – similar to Swedish meatballs – inside a wrap, this similar to a Mexican soft tortilla. It is very good. The small lamb chop and pork cops instead are not tender, and the sauces that go with it are not that good, at least to my taste. At least a couple of times during the meal, I keep on urging Elena to have a quick lunch, so I can get to the part of the day I am most looking forward to, which is the guided tour of Moscow.

Traveling really opens our mind. Ignorance is one of the biggest problems humanity has. Think of the worst characters in our history. Both Hitler and Stalin originated from small towns, traveled little, and had prejudices towards some ethnic groups which they would not have had if they had traveled and really understood and appreciated those who they later hated and persecuted, just because they represented the unknown, which we often confound with evil.

At around 15.30, with just an half an hour delay compared to the scheduled plan, I'm 'handed off,' right there is the parking lot of the Caucasian restaurant, to a guide, by the name of Olga. A black BMW, with again the same driver who took me from the airport to the hotel upon my arrival, is waiting to take us around Moscow. Even if still a 'tough' Russian guy, he reciprocates with a smile my friendly hello.

I must admit I felt very privileged having a guide just for myself, with a private chauffer. She makes me seat in the passenger seat, and herself sits in the back row, but in the middle, constantly protruding towards the front and towards my left ear. For the next three hours and more, she never stops teaching me about Russia.

We visit so many places. Unfortunately it mostly rains. Olga is relentless in her continuous explaining. We talk about culture, religion, and politics, as well. She is very excited to have us first stop at the University. This is one of the famous Seven Sisters, the skyscrapers built around Moscow by Stalin in the early 50's. The others are: two apartment buildings, two shopping complexes, and two government edifices (now two hotels). These seven 'Stalin Gothics' were constructed when the country laid in ruins, commissioned in 1947, just after World War II.

The Moscow State University is the oldest university in Russia, founded in 1755, initially with three schools, those of law, medicine, and philosophy. Now it has over 40 schools with over 40,000 students. It is the most prestigious Russian educational institution, and the most difficult to get in. It looks like it is meritocratic for the most part, because Olga says that, if you are persistent and dedicated, you might not get in initially, but you can study more for the difficult admissions exams and if you deserve it eventually you get accepted. In the main building, in the middle portion, there are classes and laboratories, while the two huge edifices on the sides are for student dormitories. The whole university is immersed in a huge green park.

Past the monumental front gardens, there is a famous Observatory platform. It has an incredible view of Moscow, even in the light rain and grey and poorly lighted afternoon. Olga describes the main buildings in front of us. On the near filed, there is the huge sport complex built for the 1980 Olympic Games. The stadium holds 100,000 spectators. There are many other large buildings, housing other sports, swimming, etc. She also points out most of the other seven sisters.

Next, we visit the nun monastery, which has some incredible, wonderful stories. Basically, over time, the female relatives of tsars often would end up here if they tried to usurp any of the power of their ruler relative. So Sophia – Peter the Great's step-mother - ended up here, as did the wives of Ivan the Terrible, Peter the Great, and others. Clearly, one can see fortress walls all around this monastery, so it could easily also be used for an upscale prison for rebellious sisters, wives, and even mothers. Many famous people are buried here too, such as Gorbachev's wife.

There are, of course, many beautiful gold gilded domes visible above the walls of the monastery, on top of the numerous churches. We watch them from across a seemingly man-made lake, probably like a moat to keep the fortress even more impossible to escape from. From our side, there is a sign, which I think is funny, with a man diving in the water, and a big red X sign over the image.

Olga is a fountain of information. As we drive again through the usual heavy traffic, she tells me a bit of history of Russia. What I had never realized is this next, very telling, story. There are Christian Orthodox churches everywhere. Olga says that Moscow used to be called, by some, the third Rome. After the fall of Rome in the late fourth century after Christ, Constantinople took over as the world capital, not just administratively but also religiously. After the fall of Constantinople in 1453, this mantle passed to Moscow. Unlike the other two cities (Rome and Constantinople), Olga says Russians hope Moscow will never fall. Interestingly, as we know, Istanbul (modern Constantinople) is 99% Muslim, while Russia has remained Christian, with innumerous golden-gilded domes everywhere to remind us.

But where did the tradition of these domes come from? Nobody knows for sure. Certainly, there are some of the biggest mines of gold in Russia, so it is not surprising that there is gold everywhere. But where did the characteristic onion-shape of the church domes come from? I heard at least four theories.

One, and the one Olga prefers, is that it is the shape of a burning candle, like the many that are lighted in church. The second is related to the local weather, as many think that this shape was chosen because it is the best to let snow fall off the domes. The third theory claims a similarity of these gilded domes to battle helmets worn by Russian soldiers in the middle ages. In fact, churches are erected here in Russia to celebrate war victories, which is certainly not a tradition of other Christian creeds. Last, some say the Russian copied the Mongols for these domes.

We get back in the car, and drive now towards the center of Moscow, which is the Kremlin. As we get close, we drive by the Bolshoi Theatre, and the KGB building. 'Bolshoi' means 'big,' and it was formerly known as the Great Imperial Theatre. It has a stately colonnade in front, and a chariot with Apollo on top. I take a picture of both of these world-famous buildings. The driver, usually a quiet man, but clearly following closely the conversation between the guide and I, jokes with me that now the police is going to arrest me, as I have taken a picture of the feared KGB building. It is closed to visitors.

We then stop at the Red Square. We can only visit St Basil from the outside. It really looks like the symbol of Russia, a place I've never seen in person before this week, but many times in pictures whenever Russia or Moscow are mentioned. This church was also built to celebrate a military victory, that of the Tartar city of Kazan by Ivan the Terrible in 1552.

Ivan the IV, called the Terrible, remains the classic Russian tyrant. He was only three years old when his father, Vasilii III, died in 1533. His mother became the regent, but was poisoned to death in 1538. For several years then, the fight for control of power in the empire caused executions, murders, exiles, and imprisonments. Ivan, who was apparently originally a sensitive, smart, and precocious boy, must have been significantly affected by the violence and schemes all around him.

In 1547, at the age of 16, Ivan decided to get crowned, not as a Grand Prince, as previous Russian rulers had been, but as a tsar, Ivan IV. The elaborate and awe-inspiring ceremony served to endow the tsar with sacred authority directly from Byzantium (Constantinople). In the same year, Ivan IV (only later called the Terrible) married Anastasia Romanov, from whose side of the family later the Romanov ruled Russia for almost 4 centuries (Table 1, page 78).

Ivan IV was responsible for defeating the Tartars, and annexing their territories, including the Kazan, Astrakhan, and the Crimea, obtaining control of the important Volga region. He also expanded the Russian territories towards Lithuania and other lands. His beloved wife Anastasia died suddenly in 1560, and he thought this was due to a plot to poison her.

From this point on, he began to fight against the aristocrats who were always trying to get some of his power, called the 'boyars.' Eventually, his became a reign of terror, including, if the reports can be believed, dismemberings, crucifixions, and skinning of his victims. In 1581, in a fit of violence, Ivan IV struck his son and heir Ivan and mortally wounded him. Interestingly, Ivan IV prayed constantly and later would seek repentance for the 4,095 who he had ordered to be killed.

Towards the end of his reign, Russia expanded even more, with the conquest of Siberia, which came not from Ivan IV, but from the Stroganoff family, who in their quest for precious fur sent an expedition of Cossacks and other volunteers, who defeated the natives and annexed eventually of Siberia.

Looking at St Basil, Olga explains to me that most Russian churches have 1, 3, 4, or 5 domes. Domes had to be 1 (God), 3 (Trinity – Father, Son, and Holy Spirit), 4 (Jesus and Trinity), or 5 (Jesus and the four apostles). St Basil has 9 domes, a central one, and 8 dedicated to a saint on whose day the Russian army won battles against the Tartars. The cathedral was built between 1555 and 1560 on the site of the earlier

Trinity Church, where the Holy Fool Vasily (Basil) had been buried in 1552.

Basil was an adversary of the tsar, publicly reprimanding Ivan the Terrible for his cruel and bloodthirsty means. However, Basil was protected from the tsar by his status of Holy Fool, and was considered by the Orthodox Church to be an emissary of God. So, ironically, Ivan the Terrible's greatest creation, officially named the Church of Intercession, has come to be commonly known by the name of his greatest adversary, St Basil.

As almost all other churches in Russia, in 1917 the cathedral was closed, and in 1929 converted to a museum dedicated to the Russian conquest of Kazan. The museum is still open, but the church has returned also to hold religious services.

In Red Square, Olga spends also some time in front of the Lenin Mausoleum, one of Russia's most famous sites. The body of Vladimir Ilyich Lenin (1870-1924) has laid here since his death, still preserved and visible, eerily so. The mausoleum is made of dark red, black, and gray granite, with a strip of black granite near the top symbolizing mourning. This is still very much a relic of Soviet times, and its austerity frightens me.

Stalin's body, originally also shown here, has now been buried, as have been the bodies of many other Soviet leaders, such as Brezhnev, Chernenko, and Andropov. Their statues are behind the mausoleum, and I would have missed them if Olga did not point them out to me. One gets a certain sense of great power by looking at this monument in the immense Red Square.

At its peak, as the Russian Empire of the tsars and the Union of Soviet Socialist Republics (USSR), Russia represented a land mass of over 8.5 million square miles, about 1/6 of the world's land surface! The Russian Federation, even if it lost about a quarter of its territory compared to when it was the USSR, remains the largest country in the world.

We then go by the Moscow River, and Olga points to me the statue of Peter the Great, 90 feet tall, huge at the steering wheel of a vessel, to celebrate his founding of the Russian Navy in the 1700's.

We also drive by a park, in Bolotnaya Square, Balchug, 2,000 feet south of the Moscow Kremlin, to see a very interesting statue, called the Children Are the Victims of Adult Vices, by Russian artist Mikhail Chemiakin. The sculptures are of thirteen bronze figures, which depict adult vices, such as alcoholism, drug addiction, prostitution, exploitation of child labor, sadism, ignorance, war, poverty, and theft, that affect children. In the center, a statue depicting indifference.

In front of these graphic and scary statues, which are kind of a background in green bronze, there are two golden children, a girl and a boy, dancing playfully. The sculpture is a call to fight for the salvation of present and future generations. While at first I'm surprised at such a stop by Olga, I actually get to appreciate this monument a lot, as I think that growing children well is one of the most important, and difficult, responsibilities we have as adults.

We then drive to the Cathedral of Christ Our Savior. It's an imposing, grandiose structure on the Moscow river, originally built here starting in 1839. It has an amazing story of destruction and reconstruction. Its story is related to the fact that an eight 'sister' skyscraper to be added to the other seven was planned by Stalin but never built. This was the grandiose Palace of Soviets, which was to replace the Kremlin as the main seat of government. It was designed to be the tallest building in the world at 1,378 feet.

The site of the Cathedral of Christ Our Savior was chosen, and so this church was demolished in 1931. But the ground was too wet to support such an enormous structure. So a swimming pool was eventually built in 1958, until, after the fall of the Bolshevik reign, the church was rebuilt in 1997. It looks great now, dominating its surroundings. Next to it, there is statue of Alexander II.

Back at the hotel, I only have time to drop my backpack, and then go to the top floor for the scheduled 7pm dinner in the panoramic restaurant. Elena is already there at a table. The view of all of Moscow is visible through the $360^0$ degree glass around and on top of us. Elena is very talkative. She is dressed still, as in the morning, with a bright and tight pinkish dress. She is a fake blond, has brown eyes, with straight hair down to before her shoulders.

I order an antipasto of salmon, and beef Stroganoff with Pushkin potatoes, to make sure I have authentic and typical Russian food. The salmon is a bit thicker and richer than what I'm used to in the US or Italy. The beef Stroganoff is simply superb. It is made with tiny strips of beef, mixed with mushrooms in a pink delicious sauce, served in the middle of the plate like a flattish cylinder, with the thin sliced baked Pushkin potatoes all around. What a delicacy!

Elena talks constantly, about everything. Regarding politics, she thinks Abramovich and his likes have stolen from the Russian people, and she and Russians really despise them. Simply, they bought at bargain prices from poor Russians shares of formerly public companies when these went private in 1991 and soon after, and became owners of some huge Russian companies which should have instead benefited the public, who was the right owner. At least, this is her view.

We talk about contraception, abortion, politics in academia, the pharmaceutical industry in Russia and its influence from abroad. She confirms that more than 90% of doctors are women, as medicine has been a preferentially woman's profession for many decades. Interestingly, male ob-gyns are very sought after, or so she says. And almost all of the most powerful leaders in ob-gyn are men, probably because women have to also look after the family and kids. Elena herself, even if a professional woman, cooks, seemingly happily, for her husband.

She travels extensively through Russia, including the Far East, for work. She often ends up even in other European countries for meetings. She has been to Italy, Switzerland, England, and other places, not bad for a young girl. I cannot guess her age, but she does have a three-year-old daughter at home, so my guess is that she is in her late twenties or early thirties.

During the delicious dinner, there are several huge downpours, to the point that one cannot see anymore the beautiful evening lights of Moscow, but only an amorphous grey, from our rooftop restaurant. At a few point during the dinner, I could smell smoke, as tobacco smoking is allowed pretty much everywhere, including restaurants, and all public places. Elena is not happy about it, too, and says the current Moscow major is trying to pass a new law to ban it.

I do not drink any alcohol, and do not order any tea either, both quite unusual behaviors in Moscow. I do learn though how to toast in Russian, which sounds like 'Nasdaroya,' and means 'with health.' I do try the tortellini-like broth she orders for me, too. She eats very little, maybe a tenth of her salad, and half of her broth. While I decline desserts, she anyway orders for her and for me a French delicacy with strawberries and whipped cream. Delicious.

After dinner, I call Paola, but get no answer. Then I take a short walk down Old Arbat, a pedestrian street which is supposed to be a popular site at night. But there are not that many people, it is after 11 pm, maybe they are inside some of the bars and restaurants, but I am too tired to check.

## May 24, Friday

Today I have a 'free morning,' before my 1:45pm train to St Petersburg. The plan is to get to the Kremlin. I had not been able to get to it before, given it was too late on Wednesday, and every Thursday, for some unknown reason (sure, go ahead, speculate something sordid and secret), it is closed.

Once again I wake up in the middle of the night, probably around 3am, and toss and turn in the darkness for a while. At 5:20am, which is an improvement from yesterday, I check the iPhone to see the time – there are no alarm clocks in Russian hotels, apparently - and decide to stay in bed, hoping eventually to fall asleep again, as I did yesterday.

Indeed, at 8am, when the alarm clock from the TV goes off, I'm in my best, deepest sleep of the night. I force myself to get up, as I have to continue to adjust to the different – 8 hours – time zone.

I shower, shave, and prepare myself to have a relaxed day without jacket and tie. Unfortunately outside, from the huge two windows in my hotel room, everything looks wet, and grey. It's cloudy, and it is either raining or it has just finished.

I go to breakfast on the second floor. The room is very elegant. Today a different young harpist, dressed in very light blue veils, is playing soothing melodies. I resist having more than yogurt and cereals. I also drink two glasses of juice: I mix about equal parts of orange juice and a special Russian dark red berry juice.

My plan is to get to the Kremlin by 9:30am or soon after, buy the ticket, and get in by entrance time at 10am. Once back in the room, 1612B, on the 16th floor, I prepare my luggage, folding even the dirty staff properly, to make sure it fits in the carry-on again. I estimate, at my return, that it will take me only about five minutes to put the last things in, such as the guides, and my laptop.

So at about five minutes after 9am I'm off. The night before, at the beginning of Old Arbat, I had spotted a Hard Rock Café' shop. Of course, that made me think of my godson and nephew Vincenzo, my sister's son, who loves Hard Rock Café' t-shirts from around the world.

So I decide to take Old Arbat to head towards the Kremlin, hoping that the Hard Rock Café' store is already open. Indeed, it is. I buy a regular, medium, classic white t-shirt for him, and, to make things even, also two black Hard-Rock café' Moscow t-shirts for my two nieces, his sisters, Margherita and Livia. I buy an extra-small and a small, hoping they all fit, and imagining that, at 15 and 16, they like them tight, as they have enviable figures.

Then I walk quickly towards the Kremlin. I know the path well, having done it before. Interestingly, I never see a black person in my whole stay in Russia. At the end of Old Arbat, I turn slightly left to join New Arbat, which I recognize. Then I go under a pedestrian tunnel, where there are always beautiful Russian girls (but they are everywhere). I see only two bums during my stay in Moscow. I notice the sign on top of some cars, TAKCN, for taxi.

Then, I pass by a newsstand, an old movie theatre, and a Metro station. Soon after, on the right, is the Russian State Library, with the statue of Dostoyevsky, which I now know is not Lenin. I have to go under another pedestrian tunnel of the Metro system, which opens then in the square where two days prior I was stuck under torrential rain, which even stained my shoes.

I'm close to the Kremlin. Olga had told me yesterday where to buy tickets. I see the entrance she pointed to is for 'staff' only, so I have to go down the stairs towards the gardens just outside the walls of the Kremlin to find the three 'trailers' of the public ticket offices. I buy a 'territory' ticket, as they are called, a general entrance pass for the Kremlin zone, for 350 rubles.

Then I have to go up a ramp of stairs, after having showed my ticket to a guard, to the actual modern glass building of the official entrance. But, at the metal detector gate, the guard points to my backpack, and gestures for me to go back downstairs to deposit it. Despite his Russian words, I understand.

I go back the ramp of stairs, and to the baggage deposit, which, thankfully, has only one lady in front of me. I do not have to pay anything, and trade my back pack for a numbered piece of red plastic, and go up back to the metal detector check point, where they let me through. I can tell people are still afraid to enter these grounds. In fact, an elated young guy, once about ten yards past the check point, yells 'Kremlin,' to signify we had made it in!

The Kremlin is much different than what I imagined. It is a walled small little city. It is a fortress with inside some palaces for the former tsars, now for the Government officials, and at least five churches. About 90% of the 142 million citizens of Russia say they are part of the Christian Orthodox Church. So the myths I had believed in for so long are undone.

First, I thought the Kremlin as one building, a big dark enemy palace. The Kremlin instead is made up of many structures, and especially several churches, inside walls, as it is an old fortress to defend its leaders from any invader.

Second, the Kremlin to me evoked political evil, Machiavellian intrigue to conquer the whole world and make it Russian and communist. Instead, the Kremlin I visited is mainly a place of religion, of worship, of clerics.

In fact, as I walked in, at least 200 or more Christian Orthodox priests were arriving. They came out of many buses dressed with long black tunics, with beards, at times long at times short, and the typical cone hats, usually a deep purple. As they neared Cathedral Square, they donned a bright red and gold big mantle.

Several of them were immersed in praying, and getting ready for some important religious event. They all lined out outside the Church of the Ascension, in a queue over 100 meters long. Later I found out that there was a mass by the Russian Christian Orthodox Patriarch in this famous church this morning.

The first building I saw inside the Kremlin was somewhat modern, made of steel and glass, huge, rectangular, with a gold double eagle on top. This is the State Kremlin Palace, a structure of glass and aluminum, built in 1961. It is the Congress Palace where the Communist Party delegates from across the USSR would meet.

It is quite impressive, beautiful in its own formal way, and I can fantasize about the meetings here. There are still a few guards around it, which harshly reprimand a Russian tourist only because she is walking in the street in front of this Palace, where apparently it is forbidden – even if there are no cars in this wide street, closed to traffic.

Then, looking at the map in the Fodor guide, I teach myself where to go. I do follow the Orthodox priests. They go up from the State Kremlin Palace. On the left, a little more up, is the even bigger, but yellow and 19th century-looking, building, the Arsenal.

The priests veer towards their right, down now towards the Assumption Cathedral (1475-1479). On the large sidewalk, instead, there are a series of small cannons, to commemorate several wars. Then there is a huge cannon, the Tsar Cannon (casted in 1586), which weighs 40 tons. This is the largest caliber of any gun in the world. It has never fired a single shot.

From right after the State Kremlin Palace, one can see the golden tops of many churches. These are the gilded domes one can see from anywhere else in Moscow from outside the Kremlin walls. You enter the Cathedral Square in between the Tsar Cannon and Ivan the Terrible Great Tower (16th-17th century) – the tallest church tower in all of Moscow. For many years, the tallest point in Moscow, with a law that disallowed building anything taller.

Roughly, as the square is quite irregular, the other three sides are occupied by the Assumption Cathedral, where all the priests are lining up, on the right. In front, there are a small side of the yellow and white Renaissance Kremlin Palace, and the Annunciation Cathedral (1484-89) practically attached to the front of it. And, to the left of the entrance, after the tower of Ivan the Terrible, the Archangel Cathedral (1505-08).

Behind the Archangel cathedral, I also saw the Tsar Bell, casted in 1733-5, enormous at over 20 feet (6.14 meters) in height, and 200 tons in weight. As it was damaged when it was still in its cast, it never rang.
I visited in some detail two of the churches, both beautiful, and with great color hand-outs inside to help explore them.

The Archangel Cathedral was used as a burial vault for Russian tsars and princes. The architecture is a mix of architectural styles, with a Greek-cross shape, Italian Renaissance façade, and five Russian domes. By order of Ivan the Terrible (1530-84), the church is full of splendid frescos. Grand Princes of Moscow and Russia up from 1246 up to 1547 are buried here. Then, in 1547, Ivan IV the Terrible became the first tsar, and his tomb, as well as those of most other tsars up to 1712, are here.

I'm very impressed, and moved, as I usually am in cemeteries. Ivan the Terrible is buried together with his sons Ivan and Fyodor in a special tsar's vault in the altar part of the cathedral. Ivan the Terrible's son Dmitri died at seven, another of Russia's unclear mysteries as to how: its tomb is under a stone canopy on the right of the entrance.

Exiting the Archangel cathedral, I see that the cathedral in front is also open. This is the Annunciation Cathedral, the private church of Russian great princes and tsars, used for domestic and familial ceremonies. Ivan III Vasilievich, father of Ivan IV Vasilievich the Terrible, laid its foundations, and after a fire it was rebuilt also by his son. Ivan the Terrible had a special entrance to it on the side, as, per Russian Orthodox Church rules, he could not enter by its main entrance, because he was married six times, and only up to three was allowed. This cathedral has six gilded domes, and rich religious relics and icons inside.

In the Assumption Cathedral, which is the Russian Orthodox main state church, the Patriarch was celebrating mass, so I could not get in without an invitation. Here all the Russian tsars were crowned. It was closed to religious services between 1917 and 1989.

Then, between the Cathedral of the Archangel and the Ascension Cathedral, one can exit the square and cross the street to a fence, under which runs the Moscow River. This oldest part of Moscow, the Kremlin, was the original settlement, and soon a fortress in the 12th century, on the north bank of the Moscow River.

Traveling you discover that, despite we pretend to be much different, we are very much alike. The Vatican, if one thinks about it, is also somewhat of a fortress, with government and religious buildings inside. The difference is all in the perceptions, in how history and media portray the place, in a more positive or a more negative way. Visiting directly these places, and trying to interpret their history without preconceptions, as objectively as possible, can bring new, and better, understanding, and dissipate legends.

On the way out, I follow the wide asphalted road between the railing on the Moscow River on my left, and the massive structure of the yellow and white Kremlin Palace on my right. I see a high fence at the end of the building, and a big black gate. A black Mercedes, with a blue horn on it, zips in it. It must contain some government officials, some of Putin's aids.

Olga told me yesterday Putin does not live here, as he has a nice house somewhere outside the Kremlin. She was happy that recently bureaucrats have discontinued constantly stopping traffic in central Moscow for official cars to reach the Kremlin quickly, and they have had instead a heliport pad built inside the fortress.

It's almost 11am, and I've seen enough. I head out the Kremlin by a different gate – the Borovitskaya Tower - from the one I got in, the Troitskaya Tower. Central Moscow is now no secret for me. I almost find the courage to stop three Soviet-looking military men and take a picture with them, but I instead head directly to pick up my backpack in the baggage claim. Then I'm off towards Old Arbat.

Along this old, now only pedestrian street, I get attracted and go in a classic tourist trap, called 'Russian Souvenirs.' The fact that my loved ones are not with me makes me even more want to buy something for them. I come out of the store a few hundred dollars poorer, with two tiny fake Fabergé's eggs and a Red Square porcelain plate.

Real Fabergé eggs were created from 1885 to 1917 by the French artist Carl Fabergé for the tsarist family, starting with Alexander III, who ordered a bejeweled egg as an Easter present for his wife. In all, about over 50 Faberge' Imperial (big) eggs were created, most ordered by Tsar Nicholas II. Two of these magnificently luxurious eggs are on display in the Armory Palace in the Kremlin, and about 42 remain in other museums and especially in private hands, while eight are missing. The Fabergé eggs have become a symbol of luxury.

Later, I see a local with a funny t-shirt; in English, it said something like "Not enough snow today in Moscow, let it snow!', probably referring to the fact, confirmed by all the Russians I have talked to, that for at least three quarters of the year Moscow enjoys abundant snow storms.

A few minutes before 12.00pm, I check out, and wait a few minutes for my next scheduled driver at the reception of the hotel, for the transfer to the railway station. Once again, black BMW, courtesy, and lots of traffic. The driver, even if he speaks no English at all, takes me all the way to the gate, number 1, where my 13.45 train is supposed to leave for St Petersburg. It is a «Sapsan», extremely modern, quiet, often running over 200kms an hour as smoothly as one can imagine.

I find a wonderful person called Anna Gregorova on the train. She is an old Armenian lady, a former teacher, going to visit her son in St Petersburg. She looks like old aunt Evelina, the sister of my father's dad, who lived in the little country village where my father was born. I am impressed that Anna's English, for a person her age – about 70 probably – is really good.

She is very proud to be Armenian. She says what ethnic group one belongs to is very important for people around these parts, and it used to be written in the USSR passports. For example, her sister married a Tartar. Her husband is Russian. She is happy, I can tell, that she thinks her only son tells people he is Armenian.

She had her son when she was 38. She is going to visit him, but does not know if that is good. Her son is still not married, and I can tell this is something she does not approve of. I tell her that, in two days, I will go to Italy to visit my mother and father. Her eyes sparkle from happiness when I tell her this. She has beautiful green eyes, which remind me of Emilia's, the nanny who used to live with us when I was growing up.

She says she thought I was Georgian, or Armenian, like her. Georgians and Armenian look alike. I accept like a compliment the fact that she thinks I look like her people. She instead is afraid she may have offended me.

She does not much approve of my living in the USA, away from my parents in Italy. She always told her son, "You are Russian, you should live in Russia." She is very inquisitive, and asks me why I want to live in America. I tell her my usual story about meritocracy, and finding my true self and happiness on the other side of the ocean. I could have told her anything else, she does not buy it. I should have stayed in

Italy, she says. I tell her I go back to Italy at least three times every year. I tell her my wife is Italian. Yes, she is also happy in America, and wants to stay there. She says, "Ah, success, success, success, but what after?" She just does not approve. She is polite, friendly, very talkative, but she clearly has very strong opinions.

She turns out to be very religious. She is Christian Baptist. We have a really wonderful conversation, until I tell her I believe that everything and everybody is an aspect of God. When I tell her I do not believe in Evil, she really turns, and states that the devil has deceived me into believing such a thing. She starts reading from the Bible, Matthew, which clearly she knows by heart, translating directly from Russian, quite well. So now she is praying for me. She is actually standing, eyes closed, saying something aloud.

I continue writing on the computer as she prays. Tver is first train stop. When a wonderful lunch arrives, I try again to make conversation, because clearly she likes to talk. Her son is 29, a lawyer. She lived for him; she says she worked and prayed for him all her life. She admits she had problems with her husband. He was a military man for the Soviet Union. They traveled everywhere in the USSR, including Siberia, the Black Sea, and the Far East. She did not like this kind of life. Only praying saved her, she says.

The courteous train staff asks me for choices of fish, vegetable or meat. I was not expecting lunch, but I am seated in first class, in wagon number one. I choose fish. They bring a nice tray, in which one of the dishes is four small bites of treated fish, salmon and cod, which I accompany with some bread. I think that's all, and I'm thankful, since I had absolutely no food on me.

To my surprise, the hostesses come back and ask again for a choice of meat, fish, or vegetable. This is the main, hot course. This time I go safe for chicken. It is indeed quite good. It has some potato puree on the side. Then they even serve a nice and rich chocolate cake, and tea. Russians drink a lot of tea. My companion next to me says she drinks hot tea threes times a day, every day.

She starts again the conversation, despite the fact that she does not approve of some my life's choices, and beliefs. While she smiles and looks like the most pleasant of persons, she has strong feelings. She says every single word in the Bible is correct. Anyone who sees it otherwise is incorrect.

This is how religion divides people. She has both the Old and New Testament in the book she is constantly touching, reading. She says Nigerian Christians are very nice. But Nigerian Muslims are not, they may seem ok, but they have evil inside them. I can't believe she says such things so openly, and with such a strong attitude, like others just do not see the truth, which she holds alone.

She does admit she oppressed her son. He needed freedom, and that is why he is in St Petersburg, both she and I realize. Then she complains about the vegetables, which in Moscow are from Turkey, and do not taste good, they have nitrates in them.

She prays and prays. She is much worse than my mother in her proselytism. In fact, my mother is very moderate compared to her. If one does not believe in exactly HER God, one is possessed by the devil. I'm like, I've been to several churches today, I even prayed, what have I done to sit next to someone who wants to convert me to God, in whom I already believe in?

The train smells like cigarette smoke, which is again an unpleasant experience. Anna offers me something sweet. I try to decline, but there is no way of saying 'no' to her, so I accept before pissing her off again. It's a piece of chocolate, a slender bar similar in shape to a Kinder, but with a taste like a Ferrero Roche. Her grandmother, when young, had to flee the Ottoman Empire because they wanted to convert them, Armenians, all Christians, to Islam.

Next stop is V Volochek. I remark again how the train is modern, quite comfortable, very quiet, super smooth, and has great service. We fly at 200km / hour most of the trip. Anna even tells me at some point an episode when she met some other religious people who were nice, but she could tell their happiness was a fake. She is clearly trying to tell me indirectly that my happiness is phony, and that I do not understand what is true and what is not.

The last two stops, before St Petersburg, are Bologoe, and then Chudovo. The wonderful train arrives at destination not only on time, scheduled at 6:10om, but even a few minutes early. My plan says that 'A driver will meet you with the nameplate «Berghella» and transfer you to the hotel «Corinthia», on Nevsky Prospect, 57, St. Petersburg.'

A driver again is waiting for me, just outside the number 1 first class car where I step out of. He is holding the name 'Berghella Vincenzo' typed prominently on his placard. He also does not speak great English, but swiftly, allowing me no chance to resist, grabs my bags, with the backpack neatly over the carry-on, and starts jetting out of the crowd.

I think that my train companion, Anna, seeing the sign, the driver with a blue suit, and the servility with whom he grabbed my luggage, must think I am really someone famous. I chuckle thinking of her face, and about the fact that I'm not famous at all, just lucky to have had so much from life.

The driver is one of the nicest looking, a very nice man in appearance and manners, indeed. His car is again a BMW, black, automatic as all the cars I've been in while in Russia. I give him a tip, as I have always done to all these wonderful people, drivers and guides, who have made my trip so special. I know the Corinthians Hotel is right on Nevsky Prospect, the main street in Saint Petersburg. It is in fact a huge boulevard, the Champs Elysees, or 5th Avenue, of St Petersburg.

In the hotel, a grand palace, I get my US passport back right away, at the check in. I get the immediate impression that here people are less strict than in Moscow. I lock, as usual, the passports and also the euros and the dollars in the safe in room 428. The cellular phone seems to work, so I inform my wife and my parents that I've safely arrived.

I have now time to spare, it's about 7pm, and it's still light outside. On my way out, the doorman at the Corinthians, a very nice, I would even say very handsome blond and blue eyes young – in his early 20's – Russian, tells me it is about two kilometers (less than a mile and a half) to the Winter Palace and the Hermitage.

I do walk around, without paying any attention to the map or to my guidebook. I just want to soak in the feeling of this town, its atmosphere. It's a marvelous thrill to be free to walk around a city where you have never been, this one full of history, where nobody knows you, and the language is a rebus.

I'm wearing only a shirt. But of course in the backpack I have a sweater, an umbrella, the travel book, and some water. The essentials. Russian women confirm to wear nice clothes, and high heels, supported by strong calves and legs.

I do walk the whole evening, enjoying the site of several beautiful, fantastic buildings. St Petersburg is a lot more European than Moscow, and has remarkable Imperial architecture. The planning and views are symmetrical, with perfect balances, and one can see how the style of Paris in construction design was taken as the example to imitate.

There are slightly more bums in St Petersburg, but I see maybe only about three in three hours of wandering along Nevsky Prospect. Nevsky comes from Neva, the main river in St Petersburg. Prospect from prospective, as major streets are straight, and give 'prospective,' in the perfectly designed St Petersburg, founded in 1703 by Peter the Great. St Petersburg is like Washington, DC, in the USA, or Brasilia, in Brazil: a city built from scratch to be the capital of a grand nation.

I see a САБВЗЙ, or Subway, and I get a tuna sandwich. Paola would be incredulous that I get my favorite sandwich even in St Petersburg. But I have no interest of sitting by myself in a restaurant. In fact, together with two cookies and an apple, I take them in a bag all the way to the end of Nevsky Street, Dvortsovaya Ploshchad, or Palace Square, where I know the Winter Palace and the Hermitage are.

It's getting cooler, and the wind has no obstacles in the immense square. I try to find a spot where to sit and eat. Next to the tall Alexander Column there is too much wind, and nowhere to sit. I head towards the Winter Palace, enormous and elegantly neoclassic with its green and white pastel colors, and sit on top of the front cement railing. Perhaps one of St Petersburg's greatest charms is these pastel colors of all the buildings.

But again, I'm too cold. I finally sit on the floor, around a little corner still in front of the main entrance of the Winter Palace. Nobody else is sitting on the marble pavement, and I'm afraid a guard may get me to leave. But, despite a few surprised looks by some passerby, I enjoy 15-20 minutes of sheer bliss, eating my sandwich, cookies, and apple, and staring at the beautiful structures in this famous square, where tsar ruled, and where so much of Russian history has taken place.

In 1905, on Bloody Sunday, palace guards shot dead hundreds of peaceful protesters in Palace Square. In October 1917, the Bolshevik stormed the Winter Palace and overthrew Kerensky's Provisional Government, the event which led to the birth of the Soviet Union, or USSR.

I begin to head back towards the hotel, but taking initially a different route, with the help of my map and the Fodor's guide. Across a bridge, I get to Alexander Pushkin Apartment Museum. What Dante is to Italy, Shakespeare to England, Goethe to Germany, Pushkin is to Russia. His most famous work is Eugene Onegin, which involves a young genteel girl falling in love with Onegin, only to get rejected, then years later rejecting Onegin when he falls in love with her. It is the ultimate tale of unrequited love.

Pushkin himself had many loves, was exiled by Tsar Alexander I for his criticism of the monarchy, and married one of the most beautiful women in Russia, Natalya Goncharova. He maintained his family of six with writing. He died in a rented room in this building after fighting a duel to defend his wife's honor, on January 27, 1837.

By the time I get back, walking slowly, to the hotel, it's 10pm. I'm super-tired, but outside it's sunny, there is more light than at 7pm, when it was cloudier. In the small park that one can see from my room's window, young children, probably 5 and 6 year old, are playing. After some writing and minimal reading, I'm in bed, and eventually, probably before midnight, asleep.

## May 25, Saturday

I wake up at 9am, I've slept like a baby, and it is sunny!! The forecast in my iPhone had said steady continuous rain for both Saturday and Sunday, but outside it's beautiful, at least from the windows. As I open the thick curtains, the sun is definitively shining in St Petersburg, even if about half the sky does have some white clouds. I'm so happy. Who says that sunny weather does not cause happiness?

The guide in Moscow said that St Petersburg has only about 30 days of sun per year; later, my local guide Svetlana said that indeed the days of sunshine are few, only 62 a year. And I've got one today, and even the evening before I snapped a few pictures of the sun peaking shyly through the clouds, to prove that I did see indeed the sun here in St Petersburg.

This city is at the same parallel as Anchorage, the capital of Alaska, and the story goes that many weren't happy that Peter the Great chose to build the capital of the tsar empire in such an inhospitable place, which only a tough guy like him could like.

I enjoy my fabulous room and its amenities, including a thick white bathrobe. As in the Moscow hotel, here also the bathroom had a bidet, which I would imagine is an import from the European loving Peter the Great, or Catherine the Great.

Both Peter the Great and Catherine the great were descendants of the Romanov family. Anastasia Romanov, the first 'royal' Romanov, was the wife of Ivan IV the Terrible. Their eldest surviving son Theodore ruled from 1584, at the death of his father, until 1598.

After that, the 'time of troubles' followed, so called because dynastic struggled occurred over who the next tsar should be, as there was no natural successor to the throne, and because of the war with the Poles, who had even occupied Moscow.

Eventually, the 16-year-old Michael Romanov was crowned tsar in 1613. He was the son of Metropolitan Philaret, who himself was the son of Anastasia's brother Nikita Romanov. Michael Romanov was therefore the grandnephew of Ivan the Terrible (bottom of Table 1, in cursive, page 78).

Peter I, called the Great, was the son of tsar Alexis, 'the Quietest One,' who was himself the son of Michael Romanov. (Table 2, page 79) Peter became co-tsar as a boy of 10, in 1682, together with his sickly older brother Ivan. In 1696, after the death of his mother, and of his brother Ivan, he effectively obtained total power over Russia, at the age of 24. He was strong and healthy, and a very imposing 6 feet 9 inches tall (2.04meters) – same even say 7 feet tall! He possessed astonishing physical vigor, and was positive, and active.

Peter wanted to be everywhere, and traveled indefatigably, and also wanted to see everything. He spent 18 months, between 1697 and 1698, in Europe, especially in the British Isles, Sweden, Prussia, some German states, Holland, and the Habsburg Empire in Austria. He turned to the West for skills, 'importing' hundreds of engineers, architects, artists, and other professionals from Europe, mostly from Holland.

When he returned, he suppressed an internal rebellion with exceptional severity, including the execution of more than a thousand persons, whose mangled bodies were exposed for all to see. He even imprisoned, as nuns, his step-mother Sophia, and his own wife Eudonia. Later in life, he also began to exceed in smoking, drinking, love-making, as well as some violent personal beating of his underlings.

Around 1700, Peter the Great began the Great Northern War against Sweden, then the biggest power in the Baltic, with systematic advances in Livonia and Estonia. So Peter the Great founded St Petersburg in 1703, near the mouth of the Neva, as a fortified outpost originally for fighting the Swedes, given his interest into moving Russia 'closer' to Europe.

I meet my guide for a tour of St Petersburg, Svetlana, perfectly on time as per plan, at 10am in the lobby, after another sumptuous breakfast. She is again probably in her mid- to late-fifties, has got another light shade of blue eyes compared to her similarly-aged colleague I had in Moscow, and is also an excellent guide, a wealth of information, and in absolute love with Russia and in particular St Petersburg, her town. She tells me later that Svetlana means 'light.'

The chauffer in the black BMW who drives us everywhere the

guide says to go is this time a Russian middle-aged brunette, also named Svetlana, quiet given her very limited English. Even as we travel towards the sites, Svetlana the guide bombards me with information regarding history, and culture. We stop by many sites, so that it is nearly impossible to recall them all, and their stories.

Alexander III succeeded to his father Alexander II in 1881, and reigned until 1894, at which time the last tsar of the Russian Empire came to power, Nicholas II. Alexander III was a strong man, both in physical strength, and conservative convictions. He was described as a 'mountain of stone.' He continued his predecessors' 'russification' of all lands in the empire, being a nationalist. He started to oppose non-Christian faiths as Islam, Buddhism, and Judaism. Under his reign, there were violent popular outbreaks against the Jews, called pogroms.

Unlike his father Alexander III, Nicholas II (ruled 1881-1917) was weak, even if he maintained faith, patriotism, a deep sense of duty, and devotion to his family. He increased russification in Finland, making them soon fiercely hostile to his regime. Prior alliances with Austria-Hungary and Germany ceased, and Russia became somewhat isolated. He lost the war against Japan in 1904-05, ceding territories, including the southern half of the island of Sakhalin.

Along the way, explaining the site from the car, Svetlana points to an elegant yellow palace, one of hundreds of beautiful neoclassic palaces which line the streets, especially Nevsky Prospect. It is the Yusupov Palace, famous because the murder of Rasputin started here. While it takes me a while to understand her initial explanation, I'm very familiar with the story and legend surrounding Grigorii Rasputin.

He was born in a village in the West Siberian Plain in 1872, and as a youth was a very tall wandering peasant, with penetrating light eyes. Because of his supposed healing powers, he eventually came in contact with the Nicholas II's family, as his son Alexi. He was the tsar's only son, and therefore the heir to the throne. He had hemophilia.

This, we now know, is an x-linked disorder, which he inherited from his mother, who was the carrier. Alexi's mother was one of the granddaughters of Queen Victoria, monarch of the United Kingdom, who is supposed to be carrying a new spontaneous mutation which then spread to most of the mayor royal houses in Europe.

Somehow, Rasputin was apparently able to prevent or treat Alexis' hemophiliac crises. The spontaneous hemorrhages that could kill him, and often caused extreme pain, would stop in Rasputin's presence. The tsar's wife, Alexandra, trusted Rasputin initially with his son, and then, extremely thankful and impressed by his magic powers, with everything going on in the palace, including politics.

Living often with the royal family, Rasputin was soon seen by Russian's aristocrats as a dangerous intruder, with too much influence over Nicholas II, also given his scandalous personal life. While he was married, Rasputin enjoyed an openly flirtatious and libertine life, having sex with many women both in court and outside. His wife, supposedly, understood, saying he was just a man who could not have enough from just one woman.

On the cold night of December 17, 1916, Rasputin was lured by conspirators to have dinner at Yusupov Palace, on the banks of the Moika River, which feeds the Neva River. In the underground of this building, the house of one of Russia's wealthiest families, Rasputin was fed cakes and drinks full of cyanide, enough to kill many men over.

To the horror of the conspirators, however, Rasputin was unaffected by their poison. So they shot him several times. Then they dumped him in the icy waters of the Neva River. When his body was later found and autopsied, the results purportedly showed that he died of hypothermia, not of cyanide or gunshot wounds. What a story!

Svetlana also points out to me from the car Vladimir Nabokov's house, where the author of the novel Lolita was born and lived at the begging of the 20th century. The guide then shows me a cathedral, and discusses the fact that there are about 400 churches in St Petersburg. I never knew Russians were so devout. Russia is really majorly influenced by its original history of taking the mantle of religion from Constantinople.

Next Svetlana explains the Yeliseev's Food Hall (Yeliseevskiy Gastronom), on Nevsky Prospect 56, a beautiful building and a famous St Petersburg landmark. Past that, she talks about the Square of the Arts, with the magnificent State Museum of Russian Art, as well as the

Mikhailovsky Theater of Opera and Ballet, and the home of the St Petersburg Philharmonic, all around this grandiose plaza.

To my delight, along Nevsky Prospect, we also stop and see Mikhailovskiy Palace, a splendid neoclassic building with Greek columns in front, also of a delicate pastel color – this time yellow. Svetlana says this was a wedding present of Tsar Alexander I to his brother Mikhail. It's not on Fodor's guide. It is a magnificent Empire-style palace with charming gardens on the banks of the Moika River, and it is now the home of the State Russian Museum. Alexander I chose Carlo Rossi, the Italian-Russian master of neoclassicism in St. Petersburg, to design the palace, one of the finest works of early 19th-century architecture in St. Petersburg.

In front of this work of art, there is a square and park with the imposing statue of Russia's greatest poet, Alexander Pushkin (1799-1837). It is impossible to underestimate Russia' love for what they considered their greatest poet.

The Grand Hotel Europe is the most expensive hotel in town, Svetlana says, combining prerevolutionary elegance with modern amenities. The guide then points out Kazan Cathedral, on a major intersection also on Nevsky Prospect. I had admired this immense structure also the day before on my casual stroll.

Now I learn that tar Paul I (reigned 1796-1801) had this Cathedral built after he saw St Peter in Rome. The front is a semi-circular colonnade, designed by Andrei Voronikhin (instead of Bernini as in St Peter's). There are statues of Russian heroes who were made saints, such as Grand Prince Vladimir, who advanced the Christianization of Russia, and Alexander Nevsky, who in the 13th century defeated the German and Swedish invaders.

As almost all Russian churches, Kazan Cathedral was closed after the 1917 Bolshevik revolution. In 1932, it became the Museum of Religion and Atheism, with emphasis on the latter. I had also admired, the day before, the statues in the front gardens, those of military leaders Mikhail Barclay de Tolly, and Mikhail Kutuzov. These were generals who saved Russia from the invasion of Napoleon's troops in 1812, one of Russia's greatest victories, which certainly changed the world.

Under Tsar Alexander I, son of Paul I and grandson of Catherine the Great, Napoleon invaded Russia in June 1812 with up to 600,000 troops, against Russia's 200,000. Napoleon's Grand Armeé received tremendous resistance from Russia's soldiers, who soon got reinforcements from other fronts. But they received tremendous defeats in several battles, at Smolensk, and then at Borodino, where 28,000 French and 40,000 Russian soldiers died in one of the bloodiest battles in history.

On September 14, 1812, Napoleon entered the Kremlin. Moscow burned down. Unable to obtain peace by the fierce tsar Alexander I and largely isolated, Napoleon had to retreat before the beginning of winter. But winter did arrive during this retreat which started only in the second half of October, and Russian peasants, Cossacks, and irregular constantly harassed the French troops.

Breakdown of transportation and supply of the Grand Armeé were some of the major reasons of its collapse. Hundreds of thousands of French soldiers died of hunger and epidemics. Only 30,000 to 50,000 of them struggled out of Russia. Eventually Napoleon was also defeated in Leipzig in 1813, and, after a brief revival in 1815, suffered his final rout at Waterloo that year.

Driving towards our next destination, Svetlana points out Stroganoff Palace. This family was extraordinarily rich because of fur trade from Siberia, and since the reign of Ivan the Terrible, they were the richest businessmen in the Tsardom of Russia. They even financed the Russian conquest of Siberia. Of course, their name is now most famous for the culinary delight, Beef Stroganoff. In the road leading to our next church, I notice and ask about the Imperial Stables, where Svetlana says over 100 carriages were always ready for the tsar and his court.

We stop at the Church of the Savior on Spilled Blood, and Svetlana the driver lets us off. Svetlana the guide quickly gets us tickets. This is not only one of the most spectacular architectural sites in St Petersburg, but also a site with an amazing history.

Architecturally, it has beautiful gilded domes, of different forms, and looks strikingly similar to St Basil in Moscow, which the architect Alfred Parland was consciously aiming to copy. I take lots of pictures, as the sun is still shining off the gold and bright colors.

Historically, this Church of the Savior on Spilled Blood was commissioned and built under the helm of Tsar Alexander III, on the site where is father, tsar Alexander II, was assassinated in 1881. The height of the cathedral is exactly 81 meters, to commemorate the year. Inside, the exact spot of the attack is still left unchanged, with a part of the railing along the Moika River and the pavement where Alexander II's carriage was going at the time of the blast.

Apparently Alexander II was not badly injured after the initial explosion, so he came down the carriage trying to help injured pedestrians. A second bomb then went off right next to him, set off by People's Will, a revolutionary organization seeking democracy in Russia. He died of bleeding. The church could not have a more evocative name.

Inside, Svetlana goes on not only to describe the hundreds of extravagant and exquisite glittering details, but also a bit of the history of St Petersburg. She recalls vividly her family stories during the siege of Leningrad, in World War II. She recalls they had as food only 125grams of bread per day per person. She seems to relive the very moment when many had decided to eat all the meager stores of bread left, but her 'granny,' as she calls her now, would say no, as she insisted they would need bread the next day, and the day after that, showing everyone hope despite the desperate situation.

The city's name was changed to the more Russia-sounding Petrograd at the beginning of World War I. It was named Leningrad in 1924, at the death of Lenin. Then it went back to St Petersburg in 1991, at the end of the USSR, by popular vote. It is now the fourth biggest city in Europe, after Paris, Moscow, and London, and has over five million residents.

Inside the church, Svetlana shows me an icon of Alexander of the Neva, or Alexander Nevsky. Prince Alexander of Novgorod became a saint and a hero because around 1240 he defeated the Germans and the Swedes, on the Neva (from where his name comes from). Peter the Great build a great monastery, called Alexander Nevsky Lavra (lavra means monastery) in his honor in 1710. Architect Voronikhin, scientist

Lomonosov, writer Dostoyevsky, and musician Tchaikovsky are buried in its Lazarus cemetery, among many of Russia's greatest men and women ever.

Inside the Church of Spilled Blood, Svetlana also shows me the Tsar Gate, or Holy Gate, a remarkable huge door completely decorated in gold bas-reliefs. Interestingly, St Petersburg is so wet that the original paintings in this church were changed to mosaics for durability.

Behind the beautiful tsar gate, left open, on can see the altar, and a great mosaic of Christos Pantocrator on the back wall. The altar is supported by four columns made of jasper, which is a precious green stone used throughout the church and in other St Petersburg landmarks, including the Winter Palace.

Svetlana also describes the ceiling. Apparently, a bomb fell on the church during World War II, but, miraculously, failed to explode, and was found incidentally lying in the main cupola years later.

As we step out of the Church of Spilled Blood, Svetlana points to the railing near the canal, identical to the railing inside the church in the spot commemorating where Alexander II was killed. We walk along the canal towards Nevsky Prospects. The guide goes on to say there are about 500 bridges in St Petersburg. It is no surprise as it was built on marshes.

In fact so many people died building this city on these wet lands that it has been said that it is built on bones, not log posts. It is also said, originally by Goethe, that St Petersburg, built on over one hundred islands on the Neva delta, and with so many bridges, is the Venice of the north. But what about Amsterdam? So many cities want to be Venice!

With Svetlana the guide, as with all guides here in Russia, we often talk about their personal lives. Her family originally comes from the Murmansk region, the most northwestern part of Russia. In fact, this region is part of Lapland, and lies almost completely north of the Artic Circle. This is where here ice-colored eyes must come from, I think.

Back in the car, we drive by Mikhailovsky castle. It was build, under the design of architect Vincenzo Brenna, by Tsar Paul I. He was the son of Catherine the Great, and despised her. He held her responsible for his father's – Peter III - death, which was true. So, once a monarch himself, he lived in terror that he would be murdered, too.

Soon after he became tsar, he dreamed that the Archangel Mikhail (Michael) instructed him to build a church on his birthplace. Paul I build actually a fortress, with the Dontanka and Moika rivers as natural barriers and protective walls around. Unfortunately, 41 days after he moved in this castle, he was assassinated by suffocation with a pillow in his own bed. Russian history is certainly not scant in famous murders.

Svetlana describes to me, as we drive by them, two other features of Mikhailovsky castle, the beautiful summer garden, with 50 fountains, and the Field of Mars where Paul loved to see his troops march, and where many revolutionaries were buried.

Next, we stop briefly on the Neva, on the exact spot where St Petersburg was first founded. Here there is still the Log Cabin of Peter the Great, the initial settlement of the new capital, and his first, small and simple, residence. It was erected in May 1703. In fact, this same weekend, St Petersburg is celebrating its 310 anniversary, with great fanfare and many events.

A few yards past Peter the Great's Log Cabin, we arrive on a spot on the Neva where a big ship is anchored, and stay parked there for a few minutes as Svetlana explains the history here. We are in front of the Cruiser Aurora, built in 1903. The Russian Navy was founded by Peter the Great, who was a great believer in maritime power, in 1696. The vessel still shows the Gus flag, an historic Russian emblem. But this ship is most famous because, in October 1917, a blank shot was blasted from it, the signal for the storming of the Winter Palace by the Bolshevik Revolutionaries.

As we drive off towards the next stop, and the guide describes the city's sites, she tells me also that for over two centuries nothing taller than the Winter Palace could be built in St Petersburg, as initially decreed by Catherine the Great.

Svetlana the driver, under strict instructions by Svetlana the guide, takes us next to Peter and Paul Fortress. This turns out to be another amazing site to visit, and we spend some time wandering through its many structures. It was the first main structure built in Sankt-Piter-Burkh, the Dutch name that Peter the Great first gave to the new city in

1703, in honor of his patron saint, St Peter.

In fact, the date on which construction began on the fortress is celebrated as the birth of the city. It was built to defend the new outpost during the ongoing Great Northern War against Sweden. Peter the Great was so successful during that war that this enormous fortress was never attacked.

He defeated the Swedish army in the battle of Poltava in 1709. In addition to territorial conquests in Estonia and other close-by territories, in 1713-14 the tsar occupied also most of Finland. Russia was in control of the Gulf of Finland, and St Petersburg was its new ever-more-powerful port, Russia's new 'window into Europe.'

Inside the thick defensive walls extending on the Neva River, there are several buildings, somewhat similarly to the Kremlin in Moscow. These include churches, as well as soldier barracks, and official military quarters. In later years the fortress served mainly as a place for executions, and as a prison, similarly to the Tower of London.

In fact, the first prisoner confined to its dungeons was Peter the Great's own son, Alexei. He was tortured to death for treason, allegedly under the tsar's supervision. Dostoyevsky, Gorky, Trotsky, and many other famous Russians were unwilling guests here. At times, such as after the December 1825 uprising, after the murder of Alexander II by People's Will in 1881, and after the 1905 revolution, the place was packed with prisoners.

The main entrance to the Peter and Paul Fortress is through St Peter's Gate. Svetlana describes the double-headed eagle on top of the gate, the symbol of Russia, borrowed from Byzantium. Just beside this main gate, there is a map of the fortress, which I study well and take a picture of. Sites are numbered, and cited in both Russian, on the left, and English, on the right.

Along the main path, on the left, we encounter a statue, with about ten tourists around it as well as on top of. It is the statue of Peter the Great himself, seated, with the typical bold and small head, and long fingers. Svetlana is a bit disgusted at the fact that some Asian tourists are sitting on his lap and taking pictures. She highly reveres this greatest of tsars. I have her take a picture of me standing next to this seated giant.

Under a tunnel past Neva Gate, going to the left towards the open waters of the Neva River through the thick walls of the fortress, the guide now shows me the plaques on the wall marking flood levels of this mighty river. The gate leads to Commander's Pier, where there is a splendid view of St Petersburg. A couple of dozens tiny identical boats are sailing nearby, I assume it's a sailing school.

Svetlana points to me the main sites visible. Then, above and to the right, she remarks on the Signal Cannon, fired every day at noon. It fired off today as we first arrived, while I was buying an ice cream and Svetlana is picking up the entrance tickets. I notice a Mongolian militia of about ten men and women, seemingly on a break for tourism despite the military clothes.

The main attraction of the fortress is the Cathedral of Saints Peter and Paul. The single gilded spire of the church has a height of 400 feet, or 120 meters, which until 1962, for over 200 years, was the tallest structure (not building) in St Petersburg by Peter the Great's wish, until a TV tower was built. The spire is identical to that of the Admiralty across the river, except that it is crowned by an angel bearing a golden cross.

But the church is even more famous as the burial grounds of tsars since Peter the Great, housed in the Grand Ducal Crypt. Peter the Great's tomb is right next to the entrance we come in from. I'm moved by it, as well as by all the other tombs. Svetlana describes many of the main tsars' graves. In particular, she leads me to the chapel of the last Romanov tsar, Nicholas II, and his family, all killed in July 1918 by the Bolsheviks.

The reign of Nicholas II had seen the formation of the first significant Marxist group in 1895 in St Petersburg, the Union of Struggle for the Emancipation of the Working Class, led by Vladimir Ulianov, known by his party pseudonym of Lenin. In 1903 the Bolshevik organization was formed, also led by Lenin. On 'Bloody Sunday,' January 22, 1905, over 130 demonstrating workers were killed by Russian police while marching toward the Winter Palace.

Poverty, and the unwillingness by the regime to make major reforms, fueled the rebellion. Local soviets, or councils, began to organize. The first Duma, or Congress, was quickly dissolved as it tried to enact reforms which the tsar disagreed on. Three more Dumas were elected, but also lasted only short periods. Terrorism began to make thousands of victims starting in 1906, counterbalanced by thousands of executions by the regime. In 1911, Prime Minister Stolypin was shot dead. The regime nonetheless remained archaic and rigid.

When the Archduke Francis Ferdinand, heir to the Habsburg throne, was assassinated by Serbian patriots on June 28, 1914, the Russian government decided to support Serbia, together with France and Great Britain, against the Austrian-Hungarian Empire and Germany, as World War I started. It was then that St Petersburg changed name to a more patriotic and less German-sounding Petrograd. The war was an immense disaster for Russia. Over 1.6 million Russians died, almost 4 million were wounded, and 2.4 million taken prisoner. By 1915, Russia was in retreat, and the economy breaking down. Food shortages, crime, and strikes, became the daily routine.

Svetlana recounts how, on April 30, 1918, the dethroned Romanov family was moved to Ipatiev House, in Yekaterinburg, on the border between Europe and Asia, and spent 78 days there. On July 16/July 17, 1918, Nicholas Romanov, his wife Alexandra, their four daughters Anastasia, Tatiana, Olga and Maria, their son Alexei, as well as their court physician Dr. Yevgeny Botkin, chambermaid Anna Demidova, cook Ivan Kharitonov, and valet Alexei Trupp, were murdered.

The execution squad was comprised of four Russian Bolsheviks and seven soldiers under the Cheka chief Yakov Yurovsky. These soldiers were Hungarians, prisoners-of-war who didn't speak Russian. They were chosen because Yurovsky feared that Russian soldiers would not shoot at Nicholas and his family, particularly at his daughters.

The firing soldiers were blindfolded as well as the condemned, leading to an inefficient and tremendously messy execution process. Other versions say that the tsar was shot, then his daughters bayoneted to death. Afterwards, the Bolsheviks took the family's bodies to an abandoned mine outside Yekaterinburg and tried unsuccessfully to blow the mine up. They then retrieved the royal bodies, burned and doused them with acid, and buried them in a pit.

Svetlana goes on to describe the story of the discovery of their bodies in 1976, initially kept secret until they were dug up in 1991 and brought back to St Petersburg. DNA samples confirmed their identity - with the Duke of Edinburgh, who is related to the Russian royal family, giving a sample.

I had heard that some of their bodies, in particular the daughter Anastasia's, were never found, and many legends existed regarding her possible survival, as well as the survival of other Romanovs. Svetlana states that Alexei's and Maria's were the bodies initially not discovered, but later located in 2007 close to where the other Romanovs had been found. Unfortunately these last two members of the murdered royal family are still not here in this chapel. She is clearly unhappy about it. She then describes the tombs and some of the history of a few more famous tsars.

The small classical structure to the right as we exit the cathedral is the Boathouse. It was erected to house a replica (the original is at the Central Naval Museum) of Peter the Great's grandfather's boat. It measures 7 meters (23 ft) by 2 meters (6 ft 7 in). This boat is legendary because Peter learned to sail the ship on waters near Moscow, and so this started his love of the sea, and therefore triggered his founding of the Russian Navy, and his great western conquests, including the land leading to the Baltic, on which St Petersburg was founded.

Peter the Great was also responsible during his long reign of many reforms. He created a Governing Senate. He reorganized the country dividing it in eleven governments, and fifty provinces. He gave the Cossacks their own administration. He tried to 'russify' all his territories. He made the Church essentially a branch of government. Overall, personal rule by the tsar remained and was reinforced as the foundation of Russian administration, as has been since, up to current times.

Peter revolutionized Russia's culture in every way. He promoted the shaving of beards, until then a sign of being Russian. He promoted a more European way of dressing, especially in his court. He founded major educational schools, including a new medical school in 1706, and reformed the calendar, to make it consistent with the rest of the

European world. He changed the Russia language to a new alphabet, simplifying the old Slavonic and adopting Arabic numerals.

We hook up again with our driver, and take off for the next marvels. As we drive by one of his statues, the guide continues to praise Francesco Bartolomeo Rastrelli, the architect responsible for the Winter Palace, but also for so many other structures in St Petersburg. Interestingly, we see in several places the symbol of the city, which includes two different anchors, one for the river and one for the sea, reinforcing the notion that this is a port city, with naval power.

The next stop is St Nicholas Cathedral. As St Nicholas is the patron saint of travelers, this church has particular meaning for sailors. It is brightly white and blue on the outside, really beautiful, shaped as a wedding cake. It is one of the few churches, of course Christian Orthodox, which stayed open even during the Soviet era. The interior is also remarkable, as Svetlana explains.

During this visit, we also talk about Russian culture, and religion. Despite being an overwhelmingly Christian Orthodox society, there are about 20 million Muslims in Russia - Tartars, Chechens, and other gents in the Caucasus, making for some unrest. She also goes on a rampage against Russian men, cold, unhelpful at home, and poor family people. She points to a young Russian man, next to his wife, and holding is probably five-year-old daughter, and says, "That that's a good man, but there are only very few like him."

We then drive by a beautiful typical grandiose St Petersburg's architecture building, the Mariinsky Theatre, white and light green, an historic theatre of opera and ballet, opened in 1860. It was the preeminent music theatre of late 19th century Russia, where many of the stage masterpieces of Tchaikovsky and other great St Petersburg natives such as Rachmaninov and Prokoviev received their premieres.

Svetlana also comments that it snowed every day for 6 months this past winter. We then stop on another street corner, where I do not see major sites. She tells me, "Count how many bridges you see from this viewpoint." I count six. She tells me there are seven visible. St Petersburg is just so beautiful, to Svetlana, but also now to me. She says that here 'music is fixed in stone.' It's her favorite saying about the city.

We then drive by other sites, including the so-called 'kissing bridge' (I thought it was in Paris on the Seine…), Yusupov Palace again where Rasputin was poisoned, and the Moika River.

The next big stop is St Isaac Cathedral. Peter the Great was born on St Isaac's day, so all St Isaac's churches are homage to him. This one is the fourth church built on this site. Tsar Alexander I commissioned the construction of this current cathedral in 1818 to celebrate the victory over Napoleon, but it took forty years to build the church, under the direction of French architect Auguste de Montferrant, who died the year the cathedral was finally consecrated, in 1858.

St Isaac Cathedral's dome is the world's third largest, after St Peter's in Rome and the Duomo's in Florence. Its interior is lavishly decorated with malachite, lazulite, marble, and other stones and minerals, while the dome required 220 pounds (100 kilograms) of gold for its gilding.

The cathedral went through some hard times, as almost all other churches in Russia. In 1917, with the revolution, it was closed to worshipping. During World War II, its dome was painted black to avoid it being targeted by enemy fire, which nonetheless she was repeated hit from, with heavy damage.

While inside this church, Svetlana goes on to tell me again of what happened in St Petersburg during its 900-day siege by Hitler in WWII. In the beautiful square in front of the cathedral, called St Isaac's Square, cabbage was cultivated, and helped keep some of the local population from starving. It's hard to imagine an agricultural field in such a famous site, around the towering statue of Nicholas I, mounted on a rearing horse.

Svetlana also describes how Lake Ladoga, the largest lake in Europe, right in the outskirts of then Leningrad, provided the only access to the besieged city because a section of the eastern shore remained in Soviet hands. Supplies were transported from Finland into the city with trucks on winter roads over the ice, and by boat in the summer. This was called the "Road of Life." Nonetheless, nearly 1.1 million civilians died from starvation, disease, or air bombardments.

She likes to conclude the tour on top of the St Isaac's cathedral, to get a 360 degrees glimpse over the whole panorama of the city, and go over the sites we have visited one last time as summary. We climb the 221 steps without problems, and get to the colonnade level.

It's raining buckets, and it's cold and a bit windy, especially on the side looking towards the East. Svetlana nonetheless is in no hurry, and continues to review with me geographic and historic facts. It's clear she is used to this inclement weather. She is outstanding.

We finish the arranged tour at around 3:30pm. Svetlana had asked me previously where I wanted to be left off, and I had said Palace Square, as I was going to visit the Winter Palace and the Hermitage. She had said she does do tours of these most famous buildings, and I'm not sure if she wants me to ask her to stay and continue. But she has been marvelous already for over five hours, non-stop, with no food, drink, or bathroom break. Plus, she has said earlier tonight there is a small celebration for one of her daughter's birthday. I think it's best to part.

I give the driver 500 rubles, and the guide 1,000 rubles, delighted of their service. Svetlana the guide, who can comment in a language I understand, accepts saying it's too much. As other guides, she leaves with me her card – I learn her full name is Svetlana Verholantseva - , hoping I'll return one day or at least send her my family and friends in the future. What she has showed me is that, while Moscow is a metropolis, it cannot compare to the magnificence of St Petersburg.

Palace Square is glorious, and calm today. Alexander Column is its 156-foot-tall centerpiece. It is the memorial to Russia's victory over Napoleon in 1812. It was commissioned in 1830 by Tsar Nicholas I in memory of his brother, Tsar Alexander I, and was designed by Auguste de Montferrant. Its column was cut from a single 650-ton piece of granite. It stands in place by the sheer force of its own weight, as there are no attachments fixing it to the pedestal. In 1832, 2,000 soldiers and 200 workmen, were required to erect it, with pulleys and ropes. On top of the column there is an angel, symbolizing peace in Europe, crushing a snake, the hated French lead by Napoleon.

Opposite the Winter Palace, on the eastern side of Palace Square, is the longest building in Europe, the General Staff Building. It was built between 1819 and 1829 by the architect Carlo Giovanni Rossi, in neoclassical style, and it is indeed made up of two identical structures connected by a monumental archway. The arch itself is another commemoration of Russia's victory over Napoleon. On top of it, there is an impressive 33-foot-tall bronze of Victory driving a six-horse chariot. The army headquarters and the ministries of foreign affairs and finance were housed here in tsarist times.

Near Palace Square there is also the golden-yellow Admiralty building, with its flashing and tall spire, near the Decembrist's Square, where roughly 3,000 army officers unsuccessfully revolted to Alexander I in December, 1825. The tsar died unexpectedly then, and his brother Nicholas I took over as ruler, with hundreds of rebels suffering execution or exile to Siberia. Given this shaky start, it is not surprising that Nicholas I's reign, which lasted until 1855, was characterized by an emphasis on "faith, tsar, and the fatherland." These principles would long remain the most influential in Russian culture.

Nicholas I remained a stanch proponent of maintaining the status quo, both in his empire, and outside Russia. His successor, Alexander II, reigned from 1855 until 1881. He abolished serfdom in 1861, liberating over 23 million of them. Almost contemporaneously, about 4 million black slaves were being liberated in the United States of America. Alexander II was also responsible for the conquest of Central Asia, including the Transcaspian region, and of the Far East, including more of the lands on Pacific coast, with Vladivostok.

So, in what is now more 'spare time' on my official travel plan, I follow Svetlana's directions and find the Winter Palace ticket office inside the grand structure. I pay the 400 rubles entrance fee, without being able to also pay for the 200 rubles 'taking photos' fee, as the Russian clerk is just too hurried to hear or understand my request. It's a blessing, because I'll be able later to take as many photos as I want inside the palace. I then deposit my backpack in the free baggage service, and take a quick bathroom break, finally.

Past the metal detector check, I find the audio guide booth, ready to get one. A man in his forties softly asks from behind me if I'd like a real guide. "Of course," I reply. We bargain on the price, he asks for 2,000 rubles, but I get it down to 1,500, still a high price, probably. Once he finds out I do not care between an English or Italian guide, he quickly chooses for Italian, tells me to wait a couple of minutes, and quickly returns with a short dirty-blond woman.

My first request with her is to get some food. I buy, after a long line during which we get to know each other, a tuna sandwich, a huge Mars bar, and some water. She asks for an espresso. I devour the sandwich, while she downs the coffee, and then I manage to carry around the bar and bottle in my pockets.

Ana, the guide, was born in 1967, in a small village, the seventh of ten kids of a very poor family. She went to city when 15, 'lived the life' (her words), was married and had a baby when 20 in 1987. Her husband was a Soviet military man even if originally a Moldavian, whom she divorced 10 years after marriage, in 1993.

She then spent very poor years after Moldavia got its independence in 1991, and has been since 1998 with another man, an Ukrainian, with whom she moved to St Petersburg in 2006. She worked for many years in the food market, making 20 euros a day despite working 13 hours. She lives about a one-hour metro ride from the center of St Petersburg.

In October 2012 she took courses to become an Italian guide. She states they were very difficult, and costed an enormity, 2,000 euros. She had lessons four times per week, and twelve different exams for each of the major sites in St Petersburg (two just for the Hermitage). She took exams in Russian, but also in Italian. At the beginning she felt she did not understand anything and was desperate. She has never been to Italy, and learned her first Italian words from the dictionary. She speaks Moldavian, Russian, Ukrainian, Romanian, and some French. She learned French also from the dictionary.

Her Italian is decent, not perfect. She actually is desperate for clients. While I pay 1,500 rubles to her 'boss,' she will only get 500 rubles from him. She has come to work today at 11am, but she only has had me as client. I met her I believe around 4pm. Her boss told me that the tour was for one hour and fifteen minutes. She kept me there until 6:30pm, and the guards almost had to kick us off. The ticket office closes at 5pm, and the Hermitage closes at 6:30pm. She was a torrent of information, as she had just finished her studies.

One thing I found a bit confusing is the distinction between the Winter Palace and the Hermitage Museum. So let me get that straight right away: the Winter Palace is the huge building built by Catherine the Great to be her (the tsar's) main residence in St Petersburg. The Hermitage Museum, originally established by Catherine as a wing of the palace, is now a museum complex made up of six buildings one after and near the other, along the Neva. Four, named the Winter Palace, Small Hermitage, Old Hermitage and New Hermitage, are partially open to the public. The other two are the Hermitage Theatre and the Reserve House. So the two entities, Winter Palace and Heritage Museum, do overlap.

The Winter Palace was commissioned in 1754 by Peter the Great's daughter Elisabeth to the Italian architect Bartolomeo Francesco Rastrelli. It was the fourth royal residence on this site, stretching from Palace Square to the Neva River. It was built in the Russian rococo style most fashionable at this time, a mix of baroque and neoclassical style. It was completed in 1762, after the death of Elisabeth, and so it was finished and first inhabited by Catherine the Great, who became tsar in that year.

It remained the official main Russian tsar residence until 1917, when Nicholas II was deposed by the Bolshevik revolution. It is monumental, clearly fit to be an Imperial palace, with an elegant exterior with 2,000 windows, and inside 1,001 rooms full of malachite, jasper, agate, gilded mirrors, and precious works of art from all over the word. In 1837, after a major fire, the interiors were revamped.

Inside the Winter Palace, there is the Hermitage Museum. It is hard – or at least it was for me – to distinguish what is just palace, and what is instead museum. The museum has over 400 exhibit halls and gilded salons. The Hermitage's name comes from Catherine the Great (1729-96), who used parts of the palace for her private apartments as places of retreat and seclusion. She wanted the best art to adorn her private apartments, and even stated that "Only the mice and I can admire all this." The Hermitage name comes from the idea of her own place to admire privately art.

Catherine II, the Great, was a German princess who had married when she was 15 Tsar Peter III, Peter the Great's grandson. Peter III had himself grown up in Prussia as his mother Anne, sister to Tsar Elisabeth who had no progeny and was another of Peter the Great daughters, had married a duke there. Peter III was crude, violent, and extremely limited mentally. General dissatisfaction with his rule led to one of the many palace revolutions which have characterized Russia's history.

In 1762, when 33 years old, Catherine the Great, smart and astute, helped the coup which deposed and later killed her husband, and became empress, bypassing the natural heir, her son Paul, born to her and Peter III in 1754, and therefore only 8 at the time. She had a natural ability to govern, and an urgent drive to control and excel at everything, working day and night. In the court of her native German principality, Catherine had grown amidst a strong French culture influence.

Between 1764 and 1775, Catherine the Great acquired some of the world's finest work of art, often in completion with other European monarchs. She frequently acquired entire private collections. These original acquisitions were housed in what is currently known as the Maly (Little) Hermitage, completed in 1770. But she kept on buying, and so did her successors. A Stary (Old) Hermitage was opened in 1783, and the New Hermitage was completed in 1852 under Catherine's grandson, Nicholas I, and opened to the public for the first time then. Until 1866, admission was by royal invitation only. To me, it is unclear were each of these parts of the Hermitage start or finish, as walking through the palace, and therefore the museum, is a continuous, uninterrupted passage from marvelous to amazing works of art, including the largest collection of paintings in the world.

Ana, the guide, and me, start our visit at the honor entrance, a beautiful staircase. There is so much lapis lazuli, and malachite, I can hardly believe it. I think of my mother, who would love a necklace with just small little balls of lapis lazuli, while here there are dozens of statues and vases each with hundreds of times the amount of this precious stone needed for ladies' jewelry. Ana begins to explain to me the history of the Palace, and how its first residents were Catherine II the Great and her husband Peter III.

On the first floor, each room is more impressive than the rest. This palace and museum have nothing to envy to the best buildings or museums anywhere in the world, including Versailles, the Louvre, or the British Museum. There is just so much to admire, one could spend days in here in awe.

The room of the throne is huge, with the chair where the tsar sat dominating the space. One can imagine visitors to the Russian monarchs being intimidated by it. This is also called the Small Throne Room or the Peter the Great Memorial Hall, and was created for Tsar Nicholas I in 1833, by the architect Auguste de Montferrant. The throne is recessed in an apse before a reredos, supported by two Corinthian columns of jasper, which contains a large canvas dedicated to Peter the Great with Minerva. The silver-gilt throne was made in London in 1731.

Next we visit the Field Marshals' Hall, built to honor Imperial Russia's greatest military leaders. The Military Gallery is instead the room where 332 portraits of the generals who took part in the Patriotic War of 1812 are impressively displayed. St George's Hall is also referred to as the Great Throne Room, and is one of the largest state rooms in the Winter Palace. It served as the palace's principal throne room, and was the scene of the most formal ceremonies of the Imperial court.

In the Pavilion hall of the Small Hermitage, there are 28 impressive crystal chandeliers, but this space is famous for housing the Peacock Clock. Ana says this is the room where Catherine the Great most liked to reside in when by herself. The clock, made in England and brought here in 1781, consists of a gilded peacock on a branch, a rooster, and an owl in a cage. It still works, and, when activated, the peacock spreads its wing, the rooster crows and turns in a circle, and the owl opens and closes its eyes. There are also several other animals around, all made of gold. I imagine how Catherine would be quite entertained by such a glittering and cute display.

We then walk through, even if I do not notice much difference in style, to the Small Hermitage, and the Old Hermitage. Ana remarks how there are over three million pieces of art in the Hermitage. There are 30 kilometers (about 19 miles) of expositions! According to Ana, but also according to several historians, including Nicholas V. Riasanovsly and Mark D. Steinberg, Catherine the Great made the country – Russia –

poor, by spending too much on all this art.

Catherine's great abilities later in life morphed, and her determination became ruthlessness, and ambition lead to vanity, making her selfish. Personally, she also had many lovers, about twenty-one known ones. Under her reign, the rebellion led by Pugachev was defeated, with him decapitated and quartered, his head stuck on a pike, and the parts of his body displayed around the capital as a warning.

She strengthened serfdom (about 50% of the entire population of her country), and the power of landlords, in a country that remained overwhelmingly rural. The gulf between the few privileged at the top and the vast majority of the citizens living in poverty became wider than ever.

While Peter the Great had solved one of the three fundamental problems of Russia's foreign relations, i.e. Sweden, Catherine the Great solved the Turkish and Polish issues. She scored victory after victory. Against the Turks, she won access to the Black Sea, including the control of Crimea, with the main port of Sevastopol. Against the Poles, she won Lithuania and Ukraine. Her reign was a culmination.

Her son Paul, as we have seen, had many reasons to despise his mother. Catherine the Great had usurped his claim to the throne, dilapidated money buying lavishly European art leaving Russia full of debts when she died, and just completely eclipsed him. In his brief reign from 1796 to 1801 (when he died of another coup), he tried very much to undo his mother's works, by banning French fashion, foreign books, and foreign travel. He was capricious and neurotic, and changed the law of succession, previously set by Peter the Great as a free selection by the reigning monarch, so that only the male primogenital son could be selected.

Ana then tells me that the Old Hermitage houses 30 rooms dedicated to Italian masters, and this is clearly her favorite part. A work by Simone Martini, one of the first of the Italian works of art, is the oldest piece in the Hermitage. We saw also several works by Beato Angelico, Caravaggio, Tiziano, Leonardo, Raffaello, and others. Ana is so excited that she asks me to take a picture of her next to some of her favorite halls and masterpieces. I think this is quite unusual for a visitor to take pictures for and of the guide, but I'm delighted of her passion for the place, and naivety.

But the Hermitage is full of paintings and sculptures from masters from everywhere in the world. We also admire Rubens' and Rembrandt's masterpieces. Watching the Prodigal son – by Rembrandt – is shed a tear, as I envision myself and my dad. The hand of the old man on the back of the returned prodigal son is feminine, to emphasize the gentle feeling of welcome back. On my seeing my parents the next day in Italy, I told them this episode.

We are way past the agreed time for the tour. But Ana does not want to leave, and wants me to be even more impressed by this Russian tour. The Heritage museum is second only to the Louvre in its collection of French art. So Ana leads me to admire, on the second floor, works by Renoir, Rousseau, Gauguin, and also by Van Gogh, my favorite. She has a story for everything. "Gauguin," she recounts, "left wife and five kids, and lived in Tahiti with another woman with whom he had other kids, but nobody talks about it, this is not written in the books."

Eventually the staff at the Hermitage corners us off, and invites as to leave, as it's almost 6:30pm and closing time is 6pm. We walk out, and I'm waiting for her to take off and leave. But she hangs on. She has time to spare, loves speaking Italian, and continues to recount her interesting life to me. Eventually, she leaves for her train, saying that in St Petersburg, "It's full of criminals, watch out."

After dinner, I continue to spend time walking around, especially on Nevsky Street. I'm actually impressed by how clean, polite, and friendly the Russians I see are. They respect the red as pedestrians. They always say 'basiba' ('thank you' in Russian). I soak up the last moments of the last evening in magnificent St Petersburg.

The whole day I've been without any cell phone signal. I spend over one hour, no exaggeration, trying to make it work, by switching it off and on. I even take out the SIM card about 4 or 5 times. I spend actually first probably 15-20 minutes just trying to find something small enough to fit in the hole to remove it, on the side of the iPhone. Finally I use a clip from my conference files.

I do not sleep well, to my surprise. I wake up at 12:56am, thinking if the wake-up call does not arrive, I'll miss my ride to the airport and therefore my plane. So I turn on again my iPhone, and set the alarm there at 6:30am. The previously set-up wake-up call from the concierge was for 6:15am, in time for my 7am ride with my last arranged driver.

Then I toss and turn for a while, until I get out of bed again at 3:32am, for another brief leak, just to do something. Curious, I even open the curtains a bit, to see if the light I saw at 11pm and even midnight the nights before is still there. But it's pretty dark outside. I force myself back to the comfortable 5-star low futon bed, and the nice white sheets. Eventually, when the wake-up call does arrive right on time at 6:15am, I'm again, as the last few mornings, dreaming in my deepest sleep.

## May 26, Sunday

Quick shower. My red 'carry-on' bag and my back pack are almost completely ready from the night before. I step down to go to breakfast at 6:34am, in perfect timing. But breakfast is closed, and the polite, as usual, jacket and tie early-40's man staffing it tells me to come back in 15 minutes, that they'll open it for me. Disappointed a bit, but still ok with catching something to eat with the few rubles I have left once in the airport, I go back to my room, 428, close the two small pieces of luggage I have, make sure nothing is left in the room, and head out to check-out.

The same man at the breakfast entrance comes out to greet me at the check-out counter. He is again very nice. I have to pay in all about 3 euros, he says, which is the local municipal tax. He says I can also pay instead 155 rubles. So I give him the rubles, the only money I spend on lodging myself during the whole stay in Russia.

He then tells me to please leave my bags there next to him so he can see them, and go ahead back one flight upstairs, where I ask politely a young waitress if I can have breakfast. She politely and with a smile lets me in, the first guest there. I eat my quick mix of two delicious cereals with some berry yogurt, accompanied by a mix of orange and grapefruit juices. It does not take me more than 5 minutes, while I look out through the huge windows at the wet Saint Petersburg morning illuminating Nevsky Prospect.

By the time I walk quickly down the stairs back to the check-out counter and my bags, the nice personnel staff tells me that 'Here is my driver.' Overall, really, I could not ask for better, smoother progression in my trip. The chauffeur walks me out the back of the Corinthian, to the, for me now usual, black, shiny, 700 series BMW, automatic, with all the perks inside, including a bottle of water, Financial Times, and 20 degree Celsius air conditioning. In fact, the 'Lucas Texeira'-look-a-like (a blond and blue-eyed Brazilian friend of mine) driver, German-looking, asks first if the temperature is ok with me.

I've spent about 20,000 rubles, seemingly a large sum, mostly in gifts (some over 1,000 rubles), tips (one 1,000 rubles and several smaller ones, 500 rubles or less), food (only one meal over 1,000 rubles). I felt best obviously spending the money for gifts for my family and relatives, and for generous tips. Giving is better than receiving, as I always say. And I've received a lot from this trip, from the organizers to the wonderful guides and drivers.

The 25 minute drive is super comfortable. The chauffer has on music by Barry White, one of my favorite singers. I see large boulevards, and magnificently laid out elegant city. I see a huge statue of Lenin just before arriving at the airport.

His 1917 revolution was due to utter poverty, despair in the losses in WWI, economic breakdown, a totalitarian regime unwilling to compromise in reforms, and ultimately shortages of bread and coal. These caused new strikes, and by now soldiers sent to suppress these revolts of late February 1917 began to fraternize with the rebels.

Nicholas II was away at the front. The Duma formed a Provisional Government, and the tsar abdicated. In the meanwhile, the Bolshevik Soviets began to organized and galvanized all over Russia. Despite the Provisional Government was very democratic and liberal, it continued the war, and continued to preside over a worsening economy.

Thanks to the new government amnesty, Lenin came back from exile in April 1917. He immediately called for all power to be passed on directly to the Soviets, an immediate end of war, nationalization of land, and its distribution to the peasants, with industries under the control of the workers' councils.

On October 25, 1917, Bolshevik 'Red Guards' took control of major streets and bridges, government buildings, railway stations, police stations, and the state bank. The Winter Palace, poorly defended and housing the ministers of the Provisional Government, was stormed the night of that same day.

The Soviet Congress approved transfer of state authority to Lenin, with Trotsky and Stalin in important positions, and all local power in the hands of local Soviets. Immediate peace to all nations was declared, and the reforms planned by Lenin started to be enacted.

Seeing this statue of Lenin still remains the visitor of the Soviet times. Two days after taking control of the Winter Palace, Lenin was made chairman of the Council of People's Commissars, Trotsky the commissar of foreign affairs, and Iosif Dzhugashvilii, better known as Stalin, assumed charge of national minorities (he was from Georgia). Lenin had high intelligence, will power, persistence, courage, and worked extremely hard.

In 1918, the peace treaty ending WWI was disastrous for Russia, which lost 26% of its population, with Ukraine, Poland, Finland, Lithuania, Estonia, and Latvia all receiving independence. In Russia, all land became state property, and was given to the people to cultivate it themselves. Moscow was again made capital. In December 1922, the USSR came into being as a federation of Russia, Ukraine, Belorussia, and Transcaucasia.

Starvation, epidemics, fighting, and executions caused the loss of up to 20 million lives, and mass emigration of 2 more million, coupled with the economic crisis of 1921-22. Lenin has a stroke in 1922, and died in 1924. Stalin became General Secretary, and soon obtained boundless powers, leading even to expulsion of Trotsky in 1929. His dictatorship lasted until 1953.

Five-year economic plans contributed to enormous improvements especially in industry, particularly heavy industry, including military arsenal buildup. Quota of production for teams and for individuals were set, with some exceeding these greatly for the love of the nation. For example, Alexei Stakhanov overfilled his daily quota by 1400% in the course of a shift hewing coal. Agriculture was collectivized.

In the meanwhile, Stalin began the so called Great Purge, eliminating almost all the prerevolutionary Soviet leaders, most of the Central Committee members, arresting over 1.5 million people, with estimates of up to 2 to 3 million people killed. During these times, the slogan for the Russian citizen from the government was, "Life has become better, life has become more joyous."

In WWII, approximately 25 million Russians died. The ones liberated in Europe after being prisoners there did all they could not to return to their motherland. After the war, Winston Churchill described an 'iron curtain' separating the USSR and its controlled countries from the rest of Europe. After Stalin's death also from a stroke, Khrushchev (1953-1964), Brezhnev (1964-1982), and Andropov (1982-1985) continued, in only very slightly different styles, traditional, hard-line Soviet communist regimes.

Gorbachev was elected general secretary of the party in 1985 at 54 years of age. The USSR was again in a deep economic crisis. He was extremely hard working and refused to drink any hard liquor, knowing well alcoholism was a major problem in his population. He began to allow open criticism from previously banned books, publications, movies, and newly-released prisoners.

Feeling a relaxation of the previous central harshness, the Berlin Wall came down in 1989, and Poland, Czechoslovakia, Hungary, Romania, Bulgaria, and East Germany witnessed the collapse of their Soviet-controlled communist regimes. Several USSR provinces, such as Lithuania, Latvia, Estonia, Kazakhstan, and others, proclaimed independence. Gorbachev received the Nobel Peace prize in 1990.

Gorbachev was arrested, and then forced to resign, on December 25, 1991, his post as secretary general of a country, the USSR, that really no longer existed. Boris Yeltin became Russia' first elected president in 1991, and privatized industry, finance, commerce, agriculture, and real estate. Vladimir Putin followed as president in 2000. In 2008 Putin's prime minister Medvedev became president, and Putin prime minister. Russia is now governed by these two, both from St Petersburg.

At the St Petersburg's airport, I have to go through six checks points: at the airport front doors at the international terminal, at 2nd airport front doors at domestic terminal number 1 after I've realized I'm at the wrong terminal, at the interminably long check-in, at passport control, at the hand luggage check, and lastly through the gate - number 11 - to get to the bus, to finally drive to the plane, taking the mobile ramp of stairs to climb on the plane.

After I was told I was at the wrong terminal, I went out and accepted the offer of a man who was clearly an illegal cab driver. But I was in a rush, and I did not have much of a choice, with no official taxis in my sight. For a 10 kilometer (6 miles) ride to the other terminal, the disheveled Russian asks for 800 rubles (about $27). Once in the cab, I bargain it down to 600, and then to 500 rubles once we find out he does not have the right change.

It is not easy to go from check point to check point, as the signs are mostly in Russian, and it is confusing distinguishing between what is the check-in gate, and what is the boarding gate. The biggest mess is at the check-in point. Rossiya, Russia's second-largest airline after Aeroflot, has five flights to check in at the same time, three for Russian destinations, one for Paris, and one for Rome, and clearly they do not have enough personnel to handle it. Only 3 check-in counters. Rome is called 'Rim' in Russian, I realize.

The line is super-long. And messy. Many try to get ahead in the queue. Lines not respected; even the toughest-looking officer is a nice guy. I notice, in the crowd, I do not know why, that Russians are either all non-married, or very few wear wedding bands. I get to the front of the line for an inquiry, and the officers tell me that the Rome flight is not being checked-in yet, 'twenty minutes.' I notice that Russian passports are similar in color – a darkish red - to European ones.

Twenty-minutes later, when I ask again, they tell me, with a coy smile 'twenty minutes.' I can see though the Paris flight, leaving twenty minutes before mine for Rome, is still boarding. So I remain towards the front of the line, and exercise patience. Eventually I see the electronic 'Boarding for Rome' sign go up behind the counters, and about two minutes later the tough-looking but friendly and nice Russian officer lets me in, the first Rome-flight passenger to be allowed through, I believe. I cannot be late, I think.

Unfortunately, my 'carry-on' does not pass the stricter rules here. The nice stewardess looks at it, tells me to put it on the balance. It 17kg, and up to 8kg are allowed. She smiles, I understand, I do not fight the situation, so my carry-on is checked for Rome. A small delay on my plans.

I panicked a bit at passport control. The female officer, with usual icy Russian blue eyes, takes a long time to check my passport. Then she turns to her right, to the other customs officer. I can see now they are looking at the visa. The look at it under some special lights, and it looks like it does not look ok to either of them.

From behind the glass, I can see that a large writing 'Russia' appears in 3D in my passport under their special lights, but it does not seem to be enough. The passport is back with the officer in front of me. The passenger next to me got through much quicker on the other line, with the officer on my left. I start to envision not being allowed to pass, sent somewhere else, delayed… who knows what else…

She then pulls out a magnifying glass, and looks through it. Her right eye is an inch away from the passport page with the visa, to check it carefully. A few interminable seconds. Then she puts it back down on the desk. 'What now?' I think. But finally she stamps my passport and my boarding pass.

I panicked big time at the check in right after the passport control. Initially, to my surprise, the first officer tells me it's ok to keep my shoes on. Most people have taken the shoes off. I go through, and the metal detector beeps. The officer behind me gestures that I have to go back and take my shoes off, put them in the rolling belt for the machine, and go through the metal detector again without shoes.

I smile at the first officer, the one who told me shoes-on was ok, as I come back and he sees me with my shoes in my hand. Then, I go through the metal detector the second time, and no beep. I retrieve then my passport and pen from the tray near the metal detector, and put them as is my usual in my shirt pocket. After I retrieve my small back-pack and shoes from the metal detector, I'm about to walk through the next door, happy I passed passport control and this other metal detector check.

Then I feel my front pants pockets. There is no wallet on the right, which I always have. I check my left pocket: there is no iPhone. Moreover, I had put also my Italian passport in this left pocket. Where are they? A loud scream goes off in my head. I must have left them at the check point before the check in! I have not used them in a while. I must have left them in the side tray of some previous metal detector check, and not picked them up.

I begin to sweat cold drops in my forehead. How am I going to go back so many steps? I tell the Russian officer closest to me the situation. He is another nice guy, perhaps in his late twenties, again with short dark blond hair and light bleu eyes, as most of them. I tell him I have to go back at least a couple of check points. He can tell I'm panicked. He tells me with a smile to sit down and wait a moment. He talks with some other officers, explain in Russian the situation.

I panicked some more. How will I get back behind passport control, and then more check points? It took me forever to go through those. Will I be on time coming back to catch the plane? More importantly, how can I 'survive' without Italian passport, wallet, credit cards? I have no money! No phone! Will all these items still be all together? Which exact set point did I leave them at?

It was not a pleasant moment. These are the times that I recall all my shortcomings. The watches I used to loose when I was a young boy. I curse myself because I had thought several times during the trip that I'd had no problems, nothing lost, all connections with guides and raids and planes and trains on time, no moments of fear. Nothing had been stolen. I was still standing, anxious, unable to sit down in the narrow steel blue-painted chairs, as previously told to do.

Then I felt my pants a bit low on my waist. While I pulled them up, I realized I had no belt. "Well, I must have made it go through the machine belt, but it must have been this one. Of course, otherwise I would have felt my pants fall down much earlier, for example while in line at the passport, visa, and boarding pass check. But I didn't."

So I step to the exit belt of the metal detector I had just passed, thinking my belt must be there. It is. And my wallet, Italian passport, and iPhone, are also in the same grey large plastic rectangular bin!! I rejoice as you cannot imagine. I look up, and say somewhat loudly, "Thank you God! Thank you GOD!!"

I show immediately to the officer that I have found all my belongings, and there is no need to organize my complicated going backwards through the check points. He smiles gently, happy for me. Once again, self-inflicted pain. The world is kind to us, but we can make it ourselves hell by our own mistakes, our own fears.

Finally at the gate, I buy some last gifts, including some caviar for my family in Pescara. My trip could not have been better. I'll see my parents today, then Istanbul for another conference, then back to Philadelphia. I'm a happy and lucky guy.

And I think: how strange and weird we Italians will seem to these Russians coming to Italy. They would seem to be entitled to dislike us, if they stop at the surface and at appearances, and fail to get to know us and our history and culture better. I'm glad I feel instead a bit more Russian now.

Across the aisle from me, there is a Russian guy, about late 30's, with a Rome guide in his lap. In my head, I wish him a wonderful trip. I've read in the guide that a famous Russian said something similar, but I rephrase it: my head is American, my heart is Italian. But I must add that my soul feels like it belongs everywhere on earth.

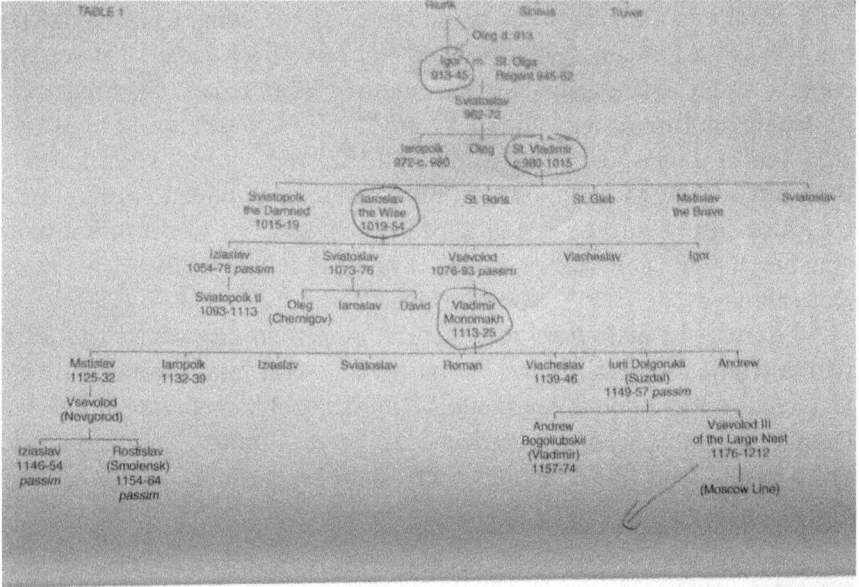

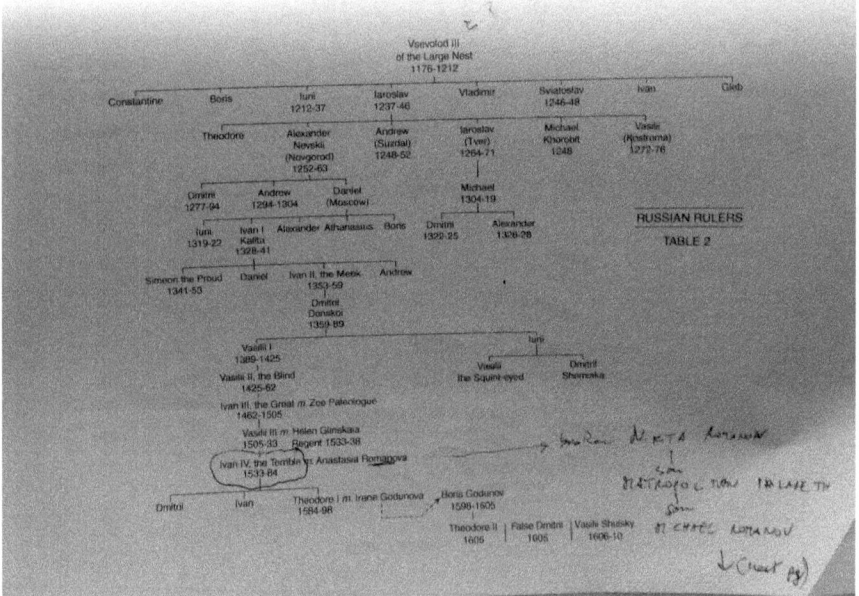

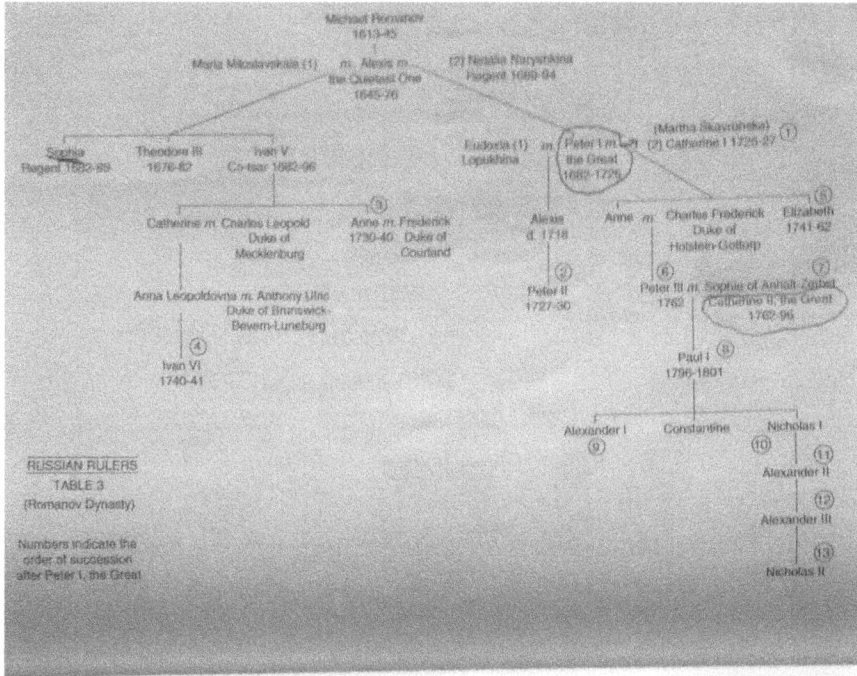

## RUSSIAN RULERS — TABLE 3 (Romanov Dynasty)

Michael Romanov
1613-45

Maria Miloslavskaia (1) m. Alexis m. (2) Natalia Naryshkina
the Quietest One
1645-76 — Regent 1680-94

Sophia Regent 1682-89 — Theodore III 1676-82 — Ivan V Co-tsar 1682-96

Eudoxia (1) Lopukhina m. Peter I m. the Great 1682-1725 (2) Catherine I 1725-27 (Martha Skavronskaia) (1)

Catherine m. Charles Leopold Duke of Mecklenburg — Anne m. Frederick 1730-40 Duke of Courland — Alexis d. 1718 — Anne m. Charles Frederick Duke of Holstein-Gottorp — Elizabeth 1741-62 (5)

Anna Leopoldovna m. Anthony Ulric Duke of Brunswick-Bevern-Luneburg — Peter II 1727-30 (2) — Peter III m. Sophie of Anhalt-Zerbst 1762 / Catherine II, the Great 1762-96 (6)(7)

Ivan VI 1740-41 (4)

Paul I 1796-1801 (8)

Alexander I (9) — Constantine — Nicholas I (10)(11)

Alexander II (12)

Alexander III (13)

Nicholas II

RUSSIAN RULERS
TABLE 3
(Romanov Dynasty)

Numbers indicate the order of succession after Peter I, the Great

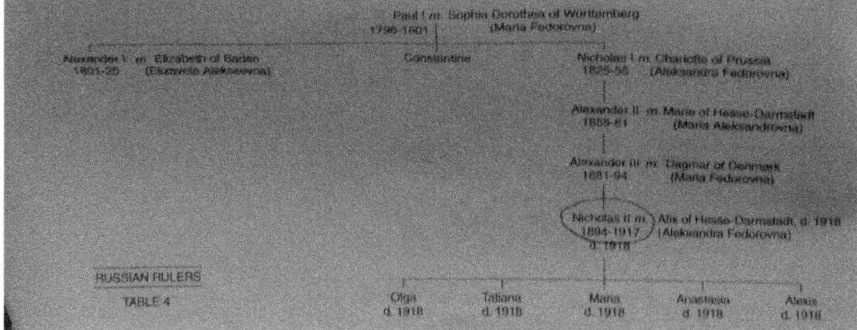

---

## RUSSIAN RULERS — TABLE 4

Paul I m. Sophia-Dorothea of Württemberg
1796-1801 (Maria Fedorovna)

Alexander I m. Elizabeth of Baden
1801-25 (Elizaveta Alekseevna) — Constantine — Nicholas I m. Charlotte of Prussia
1825-55 (Aleksandra Fedorovna)

Alexander II m. Marie of Hesse-Darmstadt
1855-81 (Maria Aleksandrovna)

Alexander III m. Dagmar of Denmark
1881-94 (Maria Fedorovna)

Nicholas II m. Alix of Hesse-Darmstadt, d. 1918
1894-1917 (Aleksandra Fedorovna)
d. 1918

Olga d. 1918 — Tatiana d. 1918 — Maria d. 1918 — Anastasia d. 1918 — Alexis d. 1918

RUSSIAN RULERS
TABLE 4

www.ingramcontent.com/pod-product-compliance
Lightning Source LLC
Chambersburg PA
CBHW021217020426

42331CB00003B/353